RACING POST
expertseries

the definitive guide to
BETTING ON FOOTBALL

kevin pullein

ABOUT THE AUTHOR

Kevin Pullein is a football writer for the *Racing Post*. His tips have shown a profit in each of the last 13 seasons, generating a total profit on turnover in excess of ten per cent. Before joining the *Racing Post*, Kevin wrote for *The Sporting Life* and was also football editor of the *Racing & Football Outlook*. He has contributed to other publications and for four seasons wrote a weekly column in the *Guardian*.

Published in 2009 by Raceform Ltd
Compton, Newbury, Berkshire, RG20 6NL

Copyright © Kevin Pullein 2009

The right of Kevin Pullein to be identified as the author of this work has been asserted by him in accordance with the Copyright, Designs and Patents Act 1988.

A catalogue record for this book is available from the British Library.

ISBN 978-1-905153-65-7

Designed by Fiona Pike
Printed in the UK by CPI William Clowes Beccles NR34 7TL

CONTENTS

FOREWORD

NOTHING BETTER SUMS UP THE IMMENSE RESPECT with which Kevin Pullein is held within the betting industry than an attempt I made to contact a friend one morning a few years ago.

My friend was a senior figure with one of the leading spread betting firms but was not answering his phone. He called me back later and apologised for not having taken my call. "We were in an emergency meeting," he revealed. "Because your man Pullein has got an edge on us on corners and we were trying to work out how to stop it."

There are some extraordinarily good sports tipsters, many of whom I have the pleasure of working with at the *Racing Post*. And then there is Kevin Pullein, who is quite simply the best football analyst and forecaster ever to have appeared in print in the UK. And if there is a better one anywhere on the planet, all I can say is he must be very good indeed.

The figures speak for themselves. Since 1996-97, when Kevin's wisdom and number-crunching first appeared in print in *The Sporting Life*, he has had an unbroken record of 13 consecutive seasons in which his staking plan has returned a profit.

That's an almost impossible feat given the expertise that his opponents – the odds-compilers – possess between them.

Frequently, the bookmaking industry has taken the attitude that if you can't beat him, employ him. But he has turned down salary offers that we at the *Racing Post* have been unable to match, mainly because he enjoys what he does, which is tipping winners.

It is not by luck that Kevin has been so successful

for so long. If they could invent an eighth day of the week he'd be even better because, like the other seven, he'd spend it working. Painstakingly collecting and inputting reams of data, refining his algorithms, watching endless hours of football, reading book after book about the game, comparing his ratings with thousands of prices in the hope of detecting an opening for profit, studying, doing all he can to be more knowledgeable, to be even better at what he does.

That's Pullein the analyst. Let me tell you a little about Pullein the man. The humble, unfeasibly courteous, friendly man. Who will unfailingly travel into London from his Hampshire home for a colleague's birthday drink. Who is always the first to email other *Racing Post* tipsters to congratulate them on a winning tip. Who continued to churn out winners and superb prose even when his wife was being treated for cancer without even a semblance of self-pity. Who is, in the eyes of all who have met him, simply a lovely guy.

You have made a wise choice buying this book. Whether it makes you a winning punter or not depends largely on what you take from it and how willing you are to accept the message that profitable betting is based on discipline, research and selectivity. What it undoubtedly will do, though, is make you a more successful punter.

BRUCE MILLINGTON
Editor, *Racing Post*

BETTING ON FOOTBALL

INTRODUCTION

THE SUCCESSFUL GAMBLER PATRICK VEITCH ONE SAID: "to win consistently, you need the odds to be wrong."

If you want to win money by betting on football, you will need to know two things. You will need to know what the odds should be, and you will need to know where you might find odds that are wrong.

The purpose of this book is to help you acquire that knowledge.

It is not easy, but if you are prepared to invest time and effort, which can still be fun, it is possible.

I hope the following pages will prove useful to all sorts of bettors, from beginners through to even some of the more experienced.

Within minutes of starting the first chapter, you will be able to form at least a broad impression of the chance of any team winning, drawing or losing against any opponents in any match that might be played in the Premier League and any division of the Football League.

By the time you have finished the first chapter, you will be able to assess with much greater accuracy the odds appropriate to contests in those competitions and many others, at home and abroad.

By the time you have finished the last chapter, you will be able to distinguish good bets from bad ones in a whole host of markets – correct score, half time/ full time result, handicap, first goalscorer and many, many more. Along the way, you might even learn one or two things you did not already know about how the game of football is played.

WHY DO YOU NEED THE ODDS TO BE WRONG?

Imagine you and I decide to bet on tosses of a coin. You can choose heads or tails. We agree to bet at even money. Every time the coin is spun, you are as likely to win as you are to lose. And when you win I will have to pay you as much money as you will have to pay me when you lose. Why bother?

Now imagine that I offer you better than even money – say, 11-10 – about your choice of heads or tails, whichever it might be. Every time you win I will pay you 11 and every time I win you will pay me 10. You can still expect to win as often as you lose, and when you win I will have to pay you more than you will have to pay me when you lose. Now you have a very good reason for bothering.

Quite simply, this is the secret of profitable betting, as easy to put into words as it is hard to put into practice. You have got to bet at odds that are bigger than they should be.

In real life, of course, I am not going to offer you 11-10. Unless their coin is dodgy, nobody is going to offer you better than even money about a spin of heads or tails, because the correct odds can be calculated precisely. It is not possible to calculate the correct odds for a sporting contest with the same precision. Opinions will differ, and for every one that is right another must be wrong. This is why it is possible to win money betting on sports.

Make no mistake about what is required, however. To win consistently you will have to reach conclusions which are different from those of the people you are betting against, and yours will have to be right and theirs will have to be wrong. Ultimately, you need to know more than they do.

WHERE ARE YOU MOST LIKELY TO FIND ODDS THAT ARE WRONG? Imagine you have walked into a shop, any shop on any high street. Which goods will be offered to you at the most attractive prices? The ones the retailer finds hardest to sell. It is the same with betting. The bets that bookmakers find hardest to sell are the ones that are most likely to represent value for money to you.

You've got to be prepared to bet on things that most people wouldn't. And what might they be? Well, they will include the bets that are least enjoyable to watch.

Suppose a game is about to be televised live on Sky. One of the things on which you could bet is whether the number of goals scored will be over or under 2.5.

If you bet on more than 2.5 goals being scored, the game will be entertaining to watch. If three goals are scored early in the first half, you can sit through the rest of the match feeling very satisfied with yourself, knowing that a profit is already in the bank. If no goals have been scored late in the second half, you can still hope for a sudden flurry of action. Your bet cannot be lost until the match is over, and while its outcome is in doubt you will always be cheering for things to happen, which is what most people like to do.

If you bet on fewer than 2.5 goals being scored, the match will be excruciating to watch. You will spend the whole 90 minutes hoping that nothing happens, or at least that not a lot happens. Every time the team in possession approaches the opposition penalty area, you will feel anxious.

Most people like to watch a match on which they

have bet. And most people like to enjoy their bet while it is in progress. So, more people will bet on over 2.5 goals than will bet on under 2.5 goals. And that is why the odds quoted for the lower total are more likely to be wrong – that is to say, wrong in your favour – than the odds quoted for the higher total.

In my opinion, the joy of winning is worth any agony that has to be endured in the process. I hope this book will help you to experience that joy more often.

SECTION 1
GOALS

CHAPTER 1

WHO WILL WIN?

"THE BEST TEAM ALWAYS WINS. THE REST IS ONLY GOSSIP." So said the late Jimmy Sirrel, who was manager of Notts County in the 1970s and 1980s as they rose from what we would now call League Two to what we would now call the Premier League.

It is not quite true, but it is close enough to being true to provide a starting point for a discussion of ways in which we can evaluate the prospects of teams winning, drawing and losing.

The biggest influence on the outcome of football matches is the abilities of the players. I estimate that 90 per cent of what happens on the pitch can be explained by the qualities of the players as revealed in the performances they have produced in the past. I will describe later how I arrived at that estimate.

What we need to be able to do is to gauge how well the two teams in a match are likely to play today. Here is a simple, subjective method that can be employed by anyone who follows football. I call it the league positions method. Ask yourself this question: if the season started afresh today, with the results of all games played so far being expunged from the record books, where in the table do you think each team would finish? I said it was simple. Just use your judgement.

And then look at **Graph 1**. It shows how the results of Premier and Football League games played during the last 14 seasons varied according to the difference in final league positions between the participants. The reason for choosing the last 14 seasons, which might sound like a strange number, is that from 1995-96 to 2008-09 there was no change in the number of teams in the Premier League or any of the three divisions of the Football League – the Championship, League One and League Two.

On top of the actual data I have superimposed what I believe to be the lines of best fit. It is something I will do repeatedly throughout this book. Real data will always jump about a bit. What we are after is the shape and direction of the underlying trends.

Suppose you are trying to appraise a game about to be played in the Premier League. You think that over a whole season team A would finish sixth and team B would finish fourteenth. In other words, you think there would be eight places separating the teams. The lines of best fit from Graph 1 suggest that if team A was playing at home there would be a 65 per cent chance of a home win, a 25 per cent chance of a draw and a 10 per cent chance of an away win. If team B was playing at home, there would be a 29 per cent chance of a home win, a 30 per cent chance of a draw and a 41 per cent chance of an away win.

Each team is more likely to win at home than away. In professional football, as is well known, teams gain an advantage from playing on their own ground. In a match between two teams of equal ability, the hosts will always be more likely winners than the visitors.

You can use the league positions method to form a general idea of the prospects of a home win, a draw and an away win in any game that might be played in the Premier League and Football League.

You will want to go further, however. You will want to assess the likelihood of different outcomes in knockout ties and also in league and cup games played in other countries. One way of doing this is to use something that I call the success rate method. It

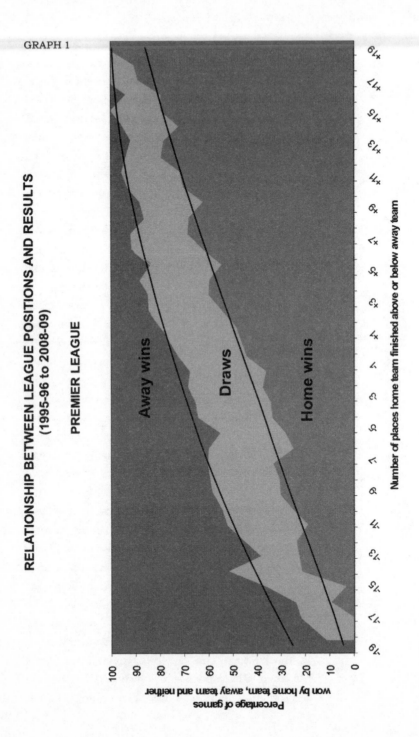

FOOTBALL LEAGUE

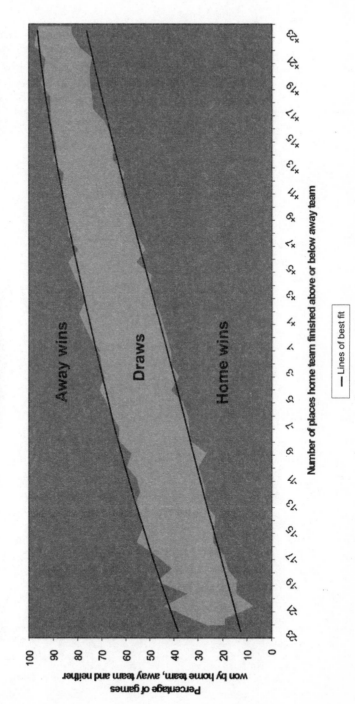

COORDINATES FOR LINES OF BEST FIT ON GRAPH 1		
Premier League		
Number of places home team finished above or below away team	Percentage of games won by home team, away team and neither	
	Home wins	Draws	Away wins
+19	86	14	0
+18	84	15	1
+17	82	16	1
+16	81	18	2
+15	79	19	2
+14	77	20	3
+13	75	21	4
+12	73	22	5
+11	71	23	6
+10	69	23	7
+9	67	24	9
+8	65	25	10
+7	63	25	12
+6	61	26	13
+5	58	27	15
+4	56	27	17
+3	54	28	18
+2	52	28	20
+1	49	28	22
-1	45	29	26
-2	43	29	28
-3	40	30	30
-4	38	30	32
-5	36	30	34
-6	34	30	36
-7	31	30	39
-8	29	30	41
-9	27	29	44
-10	25	29	46
-11	22	28	49
-12	20	28	52
-13	18	27	55
-14	15	27	58
-15	13	26	61
-16	11	25	64
-17	8	24	68
-18	6	22	71
-19	4	21	75

Football League		
Number of places home team finished above or below away team	Percentage of games won by home team, away team and neither		
	Home wins	Draws	Away wins
+23	76	20	4
+22	75	21	4
+21	74	21	5
+20	73	22	5
+19	71	22	6
+18	70	23	7
+17	69	23	8
+16	67	24	9
+15	66	24	9
+14	65	25	10
+13	63	25	11
+12	62	26	12
+11	61	26	13
+10	59	26	14
+9	58	27	15
+8	56	27	16
+7	55	27	18
+6	54	28	19
+5	52	28	20
+4	51	28	21
+3	49	28	22
+2	48	29	23
+1	46	29	25
-1	44	29	27
-2	42	30	28
-3	41	30	30
-4	39	30	31
-5	38	30	32
-6	37	30	33
-7	35	30	35
-8	34	30	36
-9	33	30	38
-10	31	30	39
-11	30	30	41
-12	28	29	42
-13	27	29	44
-14	26	29	45
-15	24	29	47
-16	23	29	49

Number of places home team finished above or below away team	Percentage of games won by home team, away team and neither		
	Home wins	Draws	Away wins
-17	21	28	50
-18	20	28	52
-19	18	28	54
-20	17	27	56
-21	16	27	58
-22	14	26	60
-23	13	26	62
Note: percentages rounded to nearest whole number			

is objective, rather than subjective, and it requires us to explore more deeply various means by which we can establish the present prowess of a team.

If a team won every game it played, it could be said to have a 100 per cent success rate. If a team lost every game it played, it could be said to have a 0 per cent success rate. If a team drew every game it played, it could be said to have a 50 per cent success rate. If we let every victory count as one, every draw as half and every defeat as zero, we can calculate a percentage success rate for any team in any competition by using this uncomplicated formula:

S = W + (0.5 x D) ÷ P x 100

In this formula, S means success rate, W means wins, D means draws and P means the number of games played. The output will always be a figure between 0 per cent and 100 per cent.

At the end of the 2008-09 Premier League season, Manchester United had won 28 games, drawn six and lost four. Altogether they had played 38 games. We can say that during the 2008-09 Premier League season the champions had a success rate of just under 82 per cent: 28 + (0.5 x 6) ÷ 38 x 100 = 81.6.

What we want to know, of course, is not how well a team has performed in the past but something that may or may not be subtly different: how well it will perform in the future.

After conducting tests on countless possibilities, I have concluded that the best estimate of how a team will perform in its next game can be obtained by weighing its performances over the last 32 games. In most divisions in most countries, this is getting on for a whole season. Arsene Wenger, the Arsenal manager, will apparently have a player watched 30 to 40 times before deciding whether to buy. He seems to think that a footballer must be observed over the equivalent of approximately a whole season for all of his strengths and weaknesses to become apparent.

I wouldn't get too hung up on a specific number: 32 games, 30 games, 40 games. If you know how well a team has performed over the last season or so, I would suggest, you already have a pretty reliable indication of how well it is likely to perform today.

Are recent results more meaningful than older ones? Yes, but don't read everything into the last few. On their own, they can be entirely meaningless.

I make myself aware of a team's results over the last 6, 12, 18 and 24 games, as well as the last 32. The last six, on their own, I would almost always ignore, no matter what they were. I consult them primarily to discover whether they are exceptionally good or bad; if they are, it is possible that some people might decide prematurely that the team is getting better or worse, and that would be worth investigating.

In most divisions in most seasons, a team that finishes in mid-table will enjoy more than one sequence of six games without a win and endure more than one sequence of six games without a loss. After six games without a victory, many people – led, no doubt, by the manager and players themselves – would think the team was getting better. After six games without a defeat, they would think the team was getting worse. Both times they would be wrong.

If a team has achieved significantly different results over the last 18 or 24 games – approximately half a season – than it has over a whole season, there would be more solid grounds for thinking it was either improving or deteriorating.

If you are ever in any doubt as to which of two success rates to expect of a team right now, choose something closer to the lower figure for a good team and something closer to the higher figure for a bad team. Former England manager Graham Taylor once said something along these lines: when you are winning you are rarely as good as they say you are, and when you are losing you are rarely as bad as they say you are. He was right. We live in a world of greys but many people see only black or white.

Are there ever any circumstances in which you should expect a team to perform in a dramatically different way in the future than it has in the past? Yes, but before you do so ask yourself some searching questions.

If a club has a new manager, ask yourself whether there are really any reasons for thinking he will do better than the old one. All clubs think their next boss will be more successful than the last one, but for every team that goes up in the standings another one goes down.

If a club has a rich new owner who is splashing money in the transfer market, ask yourself whether the players he is buying are really any better – and, if so, by how much – than the ones they are replacing.

A football team is composed of 11 players. If you change all 11, you will have a different team. When

Steven Gerrard is a good player, but Liverpool win almost as often without him

Arsenal play a youth 11 in the Carling Cup, for example, it would be daft to base your prediction of how well they will perform on the results achieved by the first 11 in the Premier League.

When a team changes a small number of players, however, the impact on performance levels is often less significant than you might think. Take the example of Steven Gerrard at Liverpool. If you asked English football followers in the summer of 2009 to name the Premier League player whose absence would have the biggest negative impact on his team, the most popular answer would probably be Gerrard. He is a totemic player. In the five seasons since Rafa Benitez became their manager, Liverpool have won 58 per cent of the Premier League games in which Gerrard started and 56 per cent of the

Premier League games in which he played no part – a difference of just two per cent.

The point here is not that Gerrard is not a good player – he is a very good player – but that even the best players, on their own, contribute less to a team than you might imagine. If Crewe Alexandra's regular right back is injured, I would suggest, you shouldn't worry over-much. If anything, people tend to over-react rather than under-react to the announcement of line-ups.

You now know enough to be able to estimate, with some accuracy, the present prowess of a team – that is to say, the success rate it can be expected to achieve from now on. If you gave a team a success rate of 65 per cent, you would effectively be saying that if it played every other team in the competition in the near future you think the success rate it achieved overall would be 65 per cent. Obviously, it would achieve a better success rate against weak opponents than it did against strong opponents. What we really want to know, then, is the success rate it can be expected to achieve against its next opponents. And we will then want to convert that figure into a percentage chance of the team winning, drawing and losing.

Look at **Table 1**. It shows the success rate selected teams can be expected to achieve when playing at home to selected opponents – or, at least, it does for games in a large number of competitions, including the English Premier and Football Leagues as well as the top divisions of Spain, Italy, Germany and France: La Liga, Serie A, Bundesliga and Le Championnat. It was calculated using formulas that, I admit, might seem a bit complicated in places, but I will give them nonetheless in a moment.

Suppose you are assessing a game about to be

SUCCESS RATE TEAM Y CAN BE EXPECTED TO ACHIEVE IN MATCHES AT HOME TO TEAM Z (%)																	
		Overall success rate expected of team Z (%)															
		10	15	20	25	30	35	40	45	50	55	60	65	70	75	80	85	90
Overall success rate expected of team Y (%)	10	59	48	39	32	27	23	19	16	14	12	10	8	6	5	4	3	2
	15	70	59	50	43	37	32	28	24	20	17	14	12	10	8	6	4	3
	20	76	67	59	52	46	40	35	31	26	23	19	16	13	11	8	6	4
	25	81	73	66	59	53	47	42	37	32	28	24	21	17	14	11	8	5
	30	85	78	71	65	59	53	48	43	38	34	29	25	21	17	13	10	6
	35	87	81	76	70	64	59	54	49	44	39	34	29	25	21	16	12	8
	40	90	84	79	74	69	64	59	54	49	44	39	34	29	24	19	14	10
	45	91	87	82	78	73	69	64	59	54	49	44	39	34	28	23	17	12
	50	93	89	85	81	77	73	68	64	59	54	49	44	38	32	26	20	14
	55	94	91	88	84	80	77	73	68	64	59	54	49	43	37	31	24	16
	60	95	92	90	87	83	80	76	73	68	64	59	54	48	42	35	28	19
	65	96	94	91	89	86	83	80	77	73	69	64	59	53	47	40	32	23
	70	97	95	93	91	89	86	83	80	77	73	69	64	59	53	46	37	27
	75	97	96	95	93	91	89	87	84	81	78	74	70	65	59	52	43	32
	80	98	97	96	95	93	91	90	88	85	82	79	76	71	66	59	50	39
	85	99	98	97	96	95	94	92	91	89	87	84	81	78	73	67	59	48
	90	99	99	98	97	97	96	95	94	93	91	90	87	85	81	76	70	59

Note: applicable to games played in Premier League, Football League, La Liga, Serie A, Bundesliga, Le Championnat and others

TABLE 1

played in League Two. You think that from now on team Y will achieve a success rate of 65 per cent and team Z will achieve a success rate of 55 per cent. Table 1 tells us that team Y can be expected to achieve a success rate of 69 per cent in matches at home to team Z. How? Run your finger down the rows on the left-hand side until it reaches 65 per cent. Now run your finger across the page – horizontally across the page – until it is in the column headed 55 per cent. The number you are pointing at is 69 per cent.

And what are the formulas? You don't need to understand how they work, but there will be times when you need to know what they are. Let S_{EHF} be the success rate team E can be expected to achieve in a match at home to team F.

$$S_{EHF} = J \div (J + K) \times 100$$

We calculate J and K by applying other formulas, which are slightly more complex:

$$J = (50 \times S_E) \div (100 - S_E) \times S_H \div 50$$

$$K = (50 \times S_F) \div (100 - S_F) \times (100 - S_H) \div 50$$

In these formulas, S_E is the overall success rate that team E can be expected to achieve from now on, and S_F is the overall success rate that team F can be expected to achieve from now on. The other term, S_H, is an average of the success rates that all teams in the competition can be expected to achieve in their home games. In the English Premier and Football Leagues, S_H is usually around 59 per cent – as it is in the top divisions of Spain, Italy, Germany and France. In the Scottish Premier League, it is usually a bit lower, but still around 56 per cent. The figure used for calculations in Table 1 was 59 per cent.

When two teams play at a neutral venue – in a cup final, for example – one of them is officially designated as the home team and the other is officially designated as the away team, but the location of the match has no bearing on the outcome, so on these occasions S_H will always be 50 per cent.

Okay, now look at **Graph 2**. It shows the relationship between the success rate of teams and the percentage of games they won, drew and lost. In our

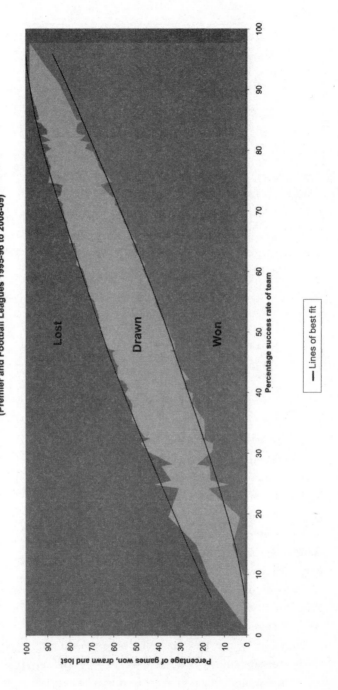

GRAPH 2

RELATIONSHIP BETWEEN SUCCESS RATE AND GAMES WON, DRAWN AND LOST
(Premier and Football Leagues 1995-96 to 2008-09)

Lost

Drawn

Won

Percentage success rate of team

Percentage of games won, drawn and lost

— Lines of best fit

SELECTED COORDINATES FROM LINES OF BEST FIT ON GRAPH 2			
Percentage success rate of team	Percentage of games		
	Won	Drawn	Lost
50	35	30	35
52	37	30	33
54	39	30	31
56	41	30	29
58	44	29	27
60	46	29	25
62	48	29	23
64	50	28	22
66	52	28	20
68	54	28	18
70	57	27	16
72	59	26	15
74	61	26	13
76	64	25	11
78	66	24	10
80	68	24	8
82	71	23	7
84	73	22	5
86	75	21	4
88	78	19	3
90	80	18	2
Note: percentages rounded to nearest whole number			

earlier example, team Y was expected to achieve a success rate of 69 per cent in League Two matches at home to team Z. **Graph 2** suggests that when team Y plays at home to team Z there will be a 56 per cent chance of a home win, a 27 per cent chance of a draw and a 17 per cent chance of an away win. Although **Graph 2** was drawn with data from games played in England, it would have looked hardly any different had it been drawn with data from games played in Scotland or many other countries, including Spain, Italy, Germany and France.

You are now in a position to be able to estimate the percentage chance of a home win, a draw and an away win in any league game that might be played

HOW SUCCESS RATE OF TEAMS ALTERED WITH PROMOTION OR RELEGATION			
(Premier League, Football League and Conference 1995-96 to 2008-09)			
Promotion			
Lower division from which team promoted	Higher division to which team promoted	Success rate during last season in lower division	Success rate during first season in higher division
Championship	Premier League	67%	39%
League One	Championship	66%	47%
League Two	League One	65%	49%
Conference	League Two	71%	51%
Relegation			
Higher division from which team relegated	Lower division to which team relegated	Success rate during last season in higher division	Success rate during first season in lower division
Premier League	Championship	32%	57%
Championship	League One	36%	52%
League One	League Two	36%	53%

TABLE 2

in a great number of countries. Or, rather, you would be if you knew how to interpret teams who move between divisions, which would also help you to evaluate cup ties.

In **Table 2**, I have given the success rates of Premier and Football League teams promoted and relegated during the last 14 seasons – in one column I have given the average success rate achieved in their last season in the old division, and in another column I have given the average success rate achieved in their first season in the new division.

We will discuss the prospects of promoted and relegated teams in more detail in Chapter 9. In the meantime, I will confine myself to a few general observations. Teams promoted and relegated between the Championship, League One and League Two all achieved an average success rate in their new division that was very close to 50 per cent – in other words, they tended to be fairly ordinary performers at their new level. Teams relegated to the Championship did better, achieving an average success rate of 57 per cent. To put this into context, however, it was still much lower than the average success rate of 67 per cent achieved by teams as they were promoted from the Championship.

You can also use **Table 2** to help you evaluate cup ties. For example, you now know that teams relegated from League One achieved a success rate of 49 per cent in League Two – so you can conclude that a better team from League One could be expected to achieve a success rate of better than 49 per cent in FA Cup ties against opponents from League Two. And so on. It is a matter of juggling the figures.

Let us go back, though, to **Graph 2**, which tells us the percentage chance in all sorts of different games of a home win, a draw and an away win. If we look very closely, we will see something very interesting. In certain types of games, the prospects of a draw are better than bookmakers' odds sometimes imply – in other words, you will sometimes be offered odds that are bigger than they should be.

Teams with a success rate between about 45 per cent and 55 per cent drew 30 per cent of their games. Table 3 tells you how to convert percentages into odds. If there is a 30 per cent chance of an event occurring, it tells us, fair odds would be somewhere between 12-5 and 9-4. For games in which a team has an anticipated success rate between about 45 per cent and 55 per cent, I can assure you, bookmakers will sometimes offer the draw at 5-2, and even 13-5. In other words, the odds will sometimes be in your favour.

Why? The best explanation is probably that very few people bet on draws. As the trading director of a very large bookmaker once told me, exaggerating

RELATIONSHIP BETWEEN PERCENTAGES AND ODDS

Percentage chance of event occurring	Fair odds	Percentage chance of event occurring	Fair odds
50.0	Evens	50.0	Evens
48.8	21-20	51.2	20-21
47.6	11-10	52.4	10-11
45.5	6-5	54.6	5-6
44.4	5-4	55.6	4-5
43.5	13-10	56.5	10-13
42.1	11-8	57.9	8-11
41.7	7-5	58.3	5-7
40.0	6-4	60.0	4-6
38.5	8-5	61.5	5-8
38.1	13-8	61.9	8-13
36.4	7-4	63.6	4-7
35.7	9-5	64.3	5-9
34.8	15-8	65.2	8-15
33.3	2-1	66.7	1-2
32.0	85-40	68.0	40-85
31.3	11-5	68.8	5-11
30.8	9-4	69.2	4-9
29.4	12-5	70.6	5-12
28.6	5-2	71.4	2-5
27.8	13-5	72.2	5-13
26.7	11-4	73.3	4-11
26.3	14-5	73.7	5-14
25.0	3-1	75.0	1-3
23.8	16-5	76.2	5-16
23.1	10-3	76.9	3-10
22.7	17-5	77.3	5-17
22.2	7-2	77.8	2-7
21.7	18-5	78.3	5-18
20.0	4-1	80.0	1-4
18.2	9-2	81.8	2-9
16.7	5-1	83.3	1-5
15.4	11-2	84.6	2-11
14.3	6-1	85.7	1-6
13.3	13-2	86.7	2-13
12.5	7-1	87.5	1-7
11.8	15-2	88.2	2-15
11.1	8-1	88.9	1-8

TABLE 3

Percentage chance of event occurring	Fair odds	Percentage chance of event occurring	Fair odds
10.5	17-2	89.5	2-17
10.0	9-1	90.0	1-9
9.5	19-2	90.5	2-19
9.1	10-1	90.9	1-10
8.3	11-1	91.7	1-11
7.7	12-1	92.3	1-12
7.1	13-1	92.9	1-13
6.7	14-1	93.3	1-14
6.3	15-1	93.8	1-15

slightly for effect: "Nobody bets on draws. Nobody places a bet unless they have a strong opinion about a match. If they think this team will win, they'll back them. If they think that team will win, they'll back them. Otherwise, they look for somewhere else to put their money." To repeat what I said in the Introduction: it is the bets bookmakers find hardest to sell that are most likely to represent value for money to you.

TABLE 3

Some time ago, if you can still recall, I estimated that 90 per cent of what happens on the football pitch can be explained by the qualities of the players, as revealed in the performances they have produced in the past. Why did I say this? For many years, I have forecast the results of league and cup games in England, Scotland and about 20 other countries round Europe. I have always observed the principles I have enunciated in this chapter. And when I compare pre-match forecasts with post-match results I find that the former explain 90 per cent of the latter.

Which suggests we should always make a small allowance for what I would call random influences, what some people would call pure luck, and what Jimmy Sirrel would have dismissed as gossip.

CHAPTER 2

HOW MANY GOALS WILL BE SCORED?

IN PRACTICE, THE LIKELIHOOD OF A GAME BEING WON, DRAWN OR LOST is influenced, to a small extent, by the likelihood of it being low scoring or high scoring. If a game is likely to be low scoring, the possibility of it being drawn goes up – and, conversely, the possibility of either team winning or losing goes down. The opposite also applies.

You will want to adjust slightly the figures you calculated in the previous chapter if you have reason to believe that a game is likely to generate either an especially small or an especially large number of goals.

And, of course, there are many other reasons why you would want to know how many goals might be scored: a great number of bets relate to how often a goalkeeper will pick the ball out of the back of a net.

The more one-sided a game is likely to be, generally speaking, the more goals there are likely to be. A lot of people would probably say: "I knew that already." A lot of people would probably overestimate how many more goals there are likely to be.

Let me explain what I mean. The average number of goals scored in Premier League games played during the last 14 seasons was just under 2.6. When teams who finished in the top three played at home to teams who finished in the bottom three, the average number of goals scored was still just under 3.0. If a cross-section of English football followers was asked how many goals were scored on average when the best teams in the Premier League played at home to the worst, most answers would probably be higher than three.

When most people overestimate the possibility of something happening, they also underestimate the possibility of the alternative happening – and the odds you are offered about the alternative happening might then be bigger than they should be.

In this chapter, we will do two things. We will discover how to work out for any match the percentage chance of no goals being scored, one goal being scored, two goals being scored, and so on. To do this we must first do something else, which is work out our goals expectation for the match. And what does that mean? Think of it this way. If these two teams played each other at this venue many times, how many goals would be scored in those games on average? The answer is our goals expectation. And what should it be?

Look at **Graph 3**. It was compiled from data on the last 14 seasons of the Premier League and Football League. It shows the relationship between the success rate of teams and the average number of goals scored in their games. On top I have superimposed a line of best fit. You will notice the previously mentioned pattern: as the difference in ability between teams increased, the average number of goals scored also increased – but it was hardly ever much higher than 3.0 or much lower than 2.5.

In the last chapter, we imagined a League Two fixture between team Y and team Z. We said that team Y should achieve a success rate of 69 per cent in matches at home to team Z. If you look at **Graph 3**, you will see that in such matches the average number of goals scored is effectively 2.6.

GRAPH 3

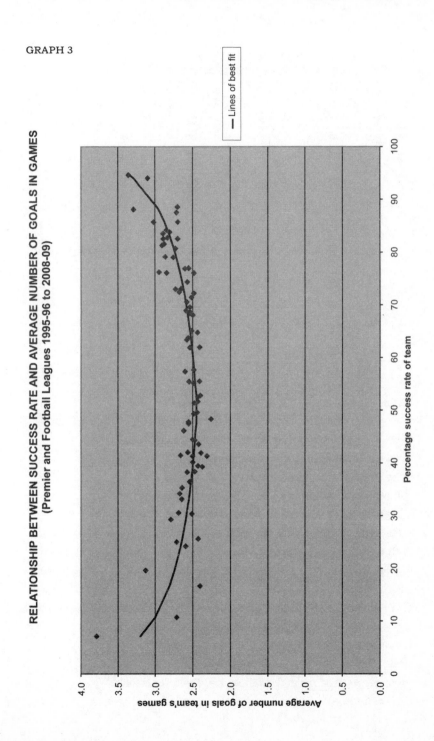

RELATIONSHIP BETWEEN SUCCESS RATE AND AVERAGE NUMBER OF GOALS IN GAMES
(Premier and Football Leagues 1995-96 to 2008-09)

Lines of best fit

Percentage success rate of team

Average number of goals in team's games

SELECTED COORDINATES FROM LINE OF BEST FIT ON GRAPH 3	
Percentage success rate of team	Average number of goals in team's games
10	3.03
15	2.85
20	2.74
25	2.65
30	2.59
35	2.54
40	2.50
45	2.47
50	2.45
55	2.47
60	2.50
65	2.54
70	2.59
75	2.65
80	2.74
85	2.85
90	3.03

So far, so good – so far, but not yet far enough. We know how many goals are usually scored in such games, but we don't know whether we should anticipate a different number in the particular game that is about to be played today between team Y and team Z.

If either or both teams had a history of featuring in games with low scores, our goals expectation should be less than 2.6. And, by the same token, if either or both teams had a history of featuring in games with high scores, our goals expectation should be more than 2.6.

We know what success rates these teams have achieved in the past, and we could find out how many goals were scored in their games. **Graph 3** would tell us whether the number of goals scored in their games was normal, high or low for a team of their calibre.

Let us suppose that the average number of goals scored in games played by team Y has been 2.8, and that the average number of goals scored in games played by teams of their standard is usually 2.5. And let us also suppose that the average number of goals scored in games played by team Z has been 2.9, and that the average number of goals scored in games played by teams of their standard is usually 2.5. In short, they have both been associated in the past with high scores.

What should we envisage today when team Y plays at home to team Z? As a rule of thumb, teams who have been involved in high scoring games in the past tend to become involved in high scoring games in the future as well – but in future their games tend to be not so excessively high scoring as they were in the past. And the same is true in reverse: teams who have been involved in low scoring games in the past tend to become involved in low scoring games in the future as well – but in future their games tend to be not so excessively low scoring as they were in the past.

So what should be our goals expectation today when team Y plays at home to team Z? According to tests I have conducted, we should give roughly three-quarters of the weight in our calculation to what usually happens in such matches and roughly one-quarter of the weight to what has been happening in the matches played by team Y and team Z. You can do that informally, by using your own subjective judgement, or you can do it formally by using this objective formula:

$$G_{YZ} = (G_M \times 0.75) +$$
$$(G_M \times (G_{YA} \div G_{YE}) \times (G_{ZA} \div G_{ZE}) \times 0.25)$$

In this formula: G_{YZ} is the goals expectation for a match about to be played between team Y and team Z; G_M is the average number of goals scored in matches of this type; G_{YA} is the average number of goals that have been scored in matches played by team Y; G_{ZA} is the average number of goals that have been scored in matches played by team Z; G_{YE} is the average number of goals usually scored in matches played by teams of the same standard as team Y; and G_{ZE} is the average number of goals usually scored in matches played by teams of the same standard as team Z.

Our goals expectation for the match about to be played between team Y and team Z then becomes:

$$G_{YZ} = (2.6 \times 0.75) + (2.6 \times (2.8 \div 2.5) \times (2.9 \div 2.5) \times 0.25) = 2.8$$

Now look at **Graph 4**. It was also compiled from data on the last 14 seasons of the Premier League and Football League. It shows the average number of goals scored in a team's games and the percentage of that team's games in which less than one goal was scored, fewer than two goals, and so on.

It tells us that when team Y plays at home to team Z there is a 6.4 per cent chance of no goals being scored, a 23.0 per cent chance of no more than one goal being scored, a 47.1 per cent chance of no more than two goals being scored, a 69.0 per cent chance of no more than three goals being scored, and so on.

We can use **Graph 4** in different ways. It tells us, for example, the percentage chance of the number of goals in a match being below or above any given total. If there is a 47.1 per cent chance of fewer than three goals being scored, for instance, there must be a 52.9

GRAPH 4

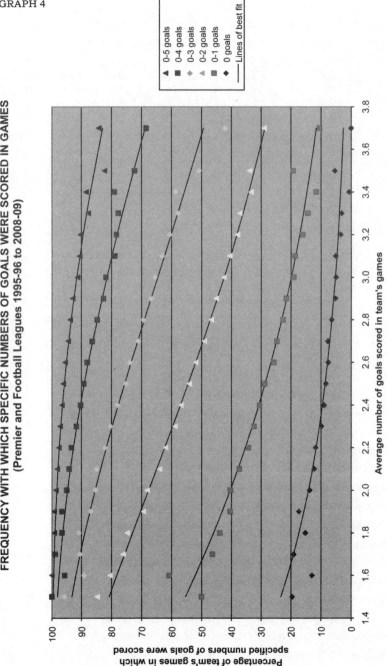

FREQUENCY WITH WHICH SPECIFIC NUMBERS OF GOALS WERE SCORED IN GAMES
(Premier and Football Leagues 1995-96 to 2008-09)

Legend:
- 0-5 goals ◀
- 0-4 goals ■
- 0-3 goals ◆
- 0-2 goals ◀
- 0-1 goals ■
- 0 goals ◆
- Lines of best fit —

X-axis: Average number of goals scored in team's games

Y-axis: Percentage of team's games in which specified numbers of goals were scored

COORDINATES FOR LINES OF BEST FIT ON GRAPH 4						
Average number of goals scored in team's games	Percentage of team's games in which specified numbers of goals were scored					
	0	0-1	0-2	0-3	0-4	0-5
1.50	23.3	55.3	80.7	93.2	98.1	99.5
1.60	21.1	52.1	78.2	91.9	97.5	99.4
1.70	19.1	49.0	75.6	90.4	96.9	99.2
1.80	17.3	46.0	73.0	88.9	96.3	98.9
1.90	15.7	43.1	70.3	87.2	95.5	98.6
2.00	14.2	40.4	67.7	85.5	94.6	98.3
2.10	12.9	37.8	65.0	83.6	93.7	97.9
2.20	11.6	35.3	62.3	81.7	92.7	97.4
2.30	10.5	33.0	59.7	79.7	91.5	96.9
2.40	9.5	30.7	57.0	77.7	90.3	96.4
2.50	8.6	28.6	54.5	75.6	89.0	95.7
2.60	7.8	26.7	52.0	73.4	87.7	95.0
2.70	7.1	24.8	49.5	71.2	86.2	94.3
2.80	6.4	23.0	47.1	69.0	84.7	93.4
2.90	5.8	21.4	44.7	66.8	83.1	92.5
3.00	5.2	19.9	42.5	64.6	81.5	91.5
3.10	4.7	18.4	40.3	62.4	79.8	90.5
3.20	4.3	17.1	38.1	60.1	78.0	89.4
3.30	3.9	15.8	36.1	57.9	76.2	88.2
3.40	3.5	14.6	34.1	55.7	74.4	87.0
3.50	3.2	13.6	32.2	53.6	72.5	85.7
3.60	2.9	12.5	30.4	51.4	70.6	84.3
3.70	2.6	11.6	28.7	49.3	68.7	82.9

per cent chance of three or more goals being scored. And so on. It can also tell us the percentage chance of any individual number of goals being scored. If there is a 47.1 per cent chance of fewer than three goals being scored and a 69.0 per cent chance of fewer than four goals being scored, it follows that there must be a 21.9 per cent chance of exactly three goals being scored (69.0 - 47.1 = 21.9). And so on.

In what kind of goal-related markets will you be offered odds that are bigger than they should be? In my experience, bookmakers sometimes underestimate how many goals are likely to be scored in a match, but many more times – overwhelmingly more often – they overestimate, and for the reason given in the Introduction. A recurring theme of this book will be that in all sorts of different ways less happens in football matches than most people realise.

Sir Walter Winterbottom, the first England manager, once said that the most important difference between football and basketball was that in the former it was so much more difficult to score than in the latter. Vive le difference, he added. It is a sentiment that has often been echoed by those who have bet on a low number of goals being scored in a football match.

CHAPTER 3

WHICH TEAM WILL SCORE FIRST?

THE REFEREE BLOWS HIS WHISTLE. The match has begun. You lean forward in your seat, watching intently. Now tell me what is happening.

A fair summary would probably be something like this: both teams are trying, with varying degrees of emphasis, to score the first goal and prevent their opponents from scoring the first goal.

If you want to know whether either of them will succeed, you will need to be able to answer two questions. Will there be a first goal? And if there is, will it be scored by this team or that team?

Let's deal with those questions in reverse order.

If there is a first goal, will it be scored by this team or that team? The better the team, the more goals it will score and the fewer goals it will concede. In other words, the higher the proportion of all goals for which it will be responsible. A team with a success rate of 50 per cent can be expected to score 50 per cent of all goals that are scored in its games. A team with a better success rate could be expected to score a higher proportion, and a team with a worse success rate could be expected to score a lower proportion. But how much higher and how much lower?

Look at **Graph 5**. It illustrates the relationship, over the last 14 seasons of the Premier and Football Leagues, between the success rate of a team and the

GRAPH 5

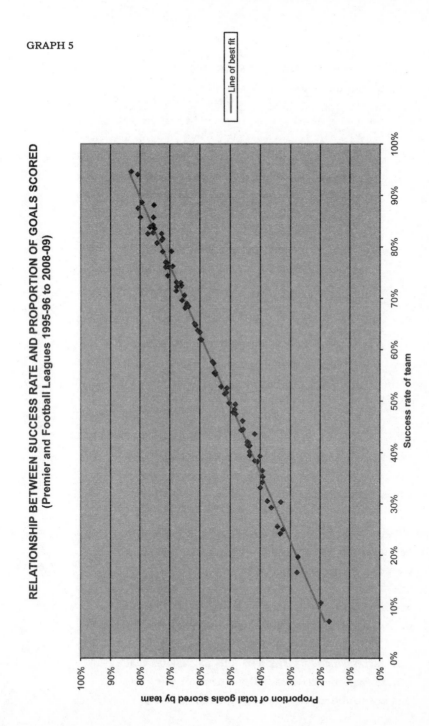

RELATIONSHIP BETWEEN SUCCESS RATE AND PROPORTION OF GOALS SCORED
(Premier and Football Leagues 1995-96 to 2008-09)

Proportion of total goals scored by team

Success rate of team

Line of best fit

SELECTED COORDINATES FROM LINE OF BEST FIT ON GRAPH 5

Success rate of team	Proportion of total goals scored by team
50%	50%
52%	52%
54%	53%
56%	55%
58%	56%
60%	58%
62%	59%
64%	61%
66%	62%
68%	64%
70%	65%
72%	67%
74%	68%
76%	70%
78%	71%
80%	73%
82%	74%
84%	76%
86%	77%
88%	79%
90%	80%

proportion of total goals scored by that team. The line of best fit was easy to draw and for most of its journey is very straight.

Let us suppose we are trying to work out what is likely to happen in a Premier League game about to be played between team Q and team R. We think team Q, which is playing at home, can be expected to achieve a success rate of 76 per cent against team R, which is playing away. Our goals expectation for the match, which will become important in a moment, is 2.6.

A quick glance at **Graph 5** tells us that team P can be expected to score 70 per cent of the goals that are scored in its game against team Q. We don't mean it will score exactly 70 per cent of the goals that are scored today – it can't unless the score is something bizarre like 7-3. We mean that if these teams played at this venue a very large number of times team Q could be expected to score 70 per cent of all the goals that were scored in those games. We can put that another way. It means there is a 70 per cent chance of team Q scoring the first goal today, if there is one.

And will there be a first goal? We can now apply again some of the knowledge we acquired in Chapter 2, in which we learnt how to work out the percentage chance of different numbers of goals being scored in a match. If you flick back to Graph 4 – it is on page 37 – you will be able to deduce that in a game with a goals expectation of 2.6 there is a 7.8 per cent chance of no goals being scored, which means there is a 92.2 per cent chance of one or more goals being scored.

We can now answer the question posed in the title of this chapter: which team will score the first goal? Apply this formula:

$$N_{QR} = (P_Q \div 100) \times T$$

The explanations are as follows: N_{QR} is the percentage chance of team Q scoring the first goal of a match against team R, P_Q is the proportion – expressed as a percentage – of all goals in the match team Q can be expected to score, and T is the percentage chance of a first goal being scored.

Applying this formula reveals there is a 64.5 per cent chance of team P scoring the first goal and a 27.7 per cent chance of team Q scoring the first goal:

$$N_{QR} = (70 \div 100) \times 92.2 = 64.5$$

$$N_{RQ} = (30 \div 100) \times 92.2 = 27.7$$

And, as we have already established, there is a 7.8 per cent chance that there will not be a first goal.

What happens if and when somebody does take the lead? You will need to know if you want to understand other markets, such as the final score and so on. And the answer might surprise you.

CHAPTER 4

HOW GOALS CHANGE GAMES

WHEN IS A TEAM AT ITS MOST EFFECTIVE? When it is losing. This might surprise you. A losing team is often thought to be playing poorly. And perhaps, up until now, it has been. But from now on, it is likely to start playing well. And this is so whether it is an ordinary team, a very good one or a very bad one.

A terrace chant often directed at the supporters of a losing team is: "You only sing when you're winning." The funny thing is that the disappointed fans who are now watching in sullen silence are likely to witness their team starting to play much better.

What I mean is that the prospect of a team scoring the next goal is higher when it is losing than when it is drawing and higher when it is drawing than when it is winning.

Graph 6 reveals how often teams score the second goal in matches where there is a second goal. It was plotted with data from the last 12 seasons of the Premier and Football Leagues, 1997-98 to 2008-09. The higher line shows how often teams scored the second goal when they were losing 0-1, and the lower line shows how often they scored the second goal when they were winning 1-0.

Let the significance of those words sink in. The higher line. Teams were more likely to score the next goal when they were losing than when they were winning. All sorts of teams – from the best, through

GRAPH 6

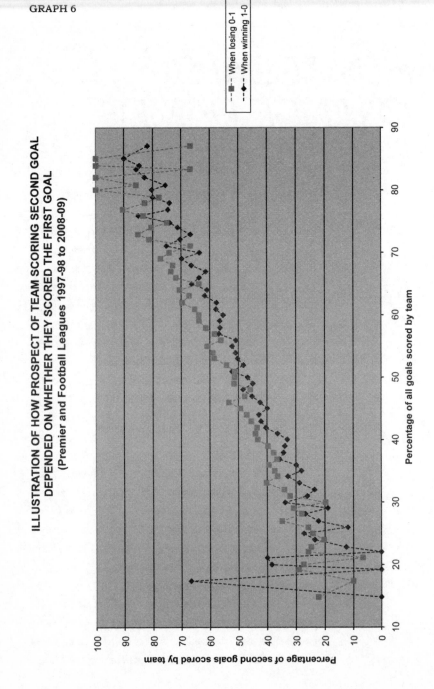

ILLUSTRATION OF HOW PROSPECT OF TEAM SCORING SECOND GOAL DEPENDED ON WHETHER THEY SCORED THE FIRST GOAL
(Premier and Football Leagues 1997-98 to 2008-09)

- When losing 0-1
- When winning 1-0

Percentage of all goals scored by team

Percentage of second goals scored by team

the mediocre to the worst.

Why should this be? It might be because teams who are trailing try harder, or because teams who are leading ease off. It might because teams who have fallen behind start to do things they were not doing before, or because teams who have gone in front stop doing things they were doing before. Or some combination of all four.

Whatever the reason, it happens. The balance of play shifts noticeably. On average, teams score the second goal six per cent more often when they are losing than when they are winning. In every match, what happens next is influenced by what has happened so far.

CHAPTER 5

WHAT WILL BE THE FINAL SCORE?

OUTSIDE THE GROUND BEFORE A MATCH, a roving television reporter will sometimes ask a group of fans for their predictions. "Four-one to Liverpool", one might shout. "Two-nil to Chelsea", another might holler in reply. Everyone thinks they know the score. Certainly, anyone who bets on football wants to know the score. So what will it be?

In this chapter, we will discuss three types of bet: the score, the number of goals gained by an individual team and the goal difference between the teams – or, handicap bets. Let's start with the middle one, the number of goals gained by an individual team.

You can already estimate how many goals will be scored in a match and what proportion will be scored by each team. You can go on very easily to establish a goals expectation for each team.

In Chapter 3 we imagined a Premier League match in which team Q was likely to score 70 per cent of all goals and team R was likely to score 30 per cent of all goals. Our goals expectation for the whole match was 2.6. Our goals expectation for team Q would be 1.8 and our goals expectation for team R would be 0.8 (70 ÷ 100 x 2.6 = 1.8, and 30 ÷ 100 x 2.6 = 0.8).

We are saying that if these teams played each other at this location a great number of times we think the average number of goals scored by team Q would

GRAPH 7

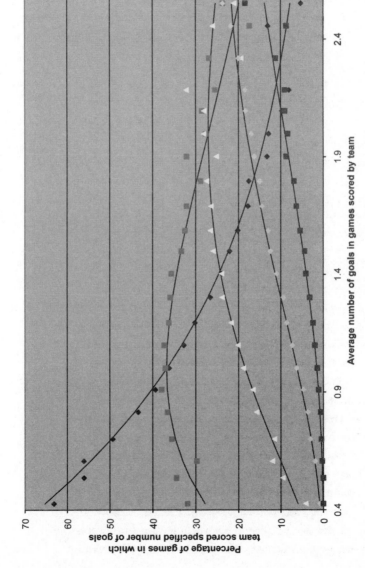

FREQUENCY WITH WHICH TEAMS SCORED SPECIFIC NUMBERS OF GOALS
(Premier and Football Leagues 1995-96 to 2008-09)

COORDINATES FOR LINES OF BEST FIT ON GRAPH 7					
Average number of goals in games scored by team	Percentage of games in which team scored specified number of goals				
	0	1	2	3	4
0.4	67	27	5	1	0
0.5	61	30	8	1	0
0.6	55	33	10	2	0
0.7	50	35	12	3	0
0.8	45	36	14	4	1
0.9	41	37	16	5	1
1.0	37	37	18	6	2
1.1	33	37	20	7	2
1.2	30	36	22	9	3
1.3	27	35	23	10	3
1.4	25	35	24	11	4
1.5	22	33	25	13	5
1.6	20	32	26	14	6
1.7	18	31	26	15	6
1.8	17	30	27	16	7
1.9	15	28	27	17	8
2.0	14	27	27	18	9
2.1	12	26	27	19	10
2.2	11	24	27	20	11
2.3	10	23	27	20	12
2.4	9	22	26	21	13
2.5	8	21	26	21	13
2.6	7	19	25	22	14

be 1.8 and the average number of goals scored by team R would be 0.8. What we really want to know, of course, is the likelihood today of them scoring no goals, exactly one goal, exactly two goals and so on.

Graph 7 tells us. It shows the relationship between the average number of goals scored by teams and the percentage of games in which they scored no goals, one goal, two goals, three goals and so on. It was compiled with data from the last 14 seasons of the Premier and Football Leagues, 1995-96 to 2008-09.

It might look like an abstract painting but it serves a concrete purpose. We can deduce that for team Q there is a 17 per cent chance of scoring no goals, a 30 per cent chance of scoring one goal, a 27 per cent chance of scoring two goals, a 16 per cent chance of scoring three goals and a seven per cent chance of scoring four goals. We can also deduce that for team R there is a 45 per cent chance of scoring no goals, a 36 per cent chance of scoring one goal, a 14 per cent chance of scoring two goals, a four per cent chance of scoring three goals and a 1 per cent chance of scoring four goals.

What is the percentage chance of the match finishing, say, 1-1? It cannot be computed very simply from the percentage chance of team Q scoring one goal and the percentage chance of team R scoring one goal. You will understand why if you think back to the last chapter.

If team Q is losing at any time during the match it becomes more likely than it would otherwise have been to score the next goal. And if team R is losing at any time during the match it becomes more likely than it would otherwise have been to score the next goal. Throughout every football match, there is in operation a kind of centripetal force that is constantly trying to pull the scores back toward the middle, or a tie.

If, at the end of the match, team Q has scored one goal, team R is more likely to have scored one goal than it would have been if team Q had scored any other number of goals. In other words, the percentage chance of team R scoring a given number of goals varies depending on how many team Q scores. And the percentage chance of team Q scoring a given number of goals varies depending on how many team R scores. So is there a way that is not too complicated in which you can assess the prospects of particular scores? Try this.

The commonest winning score is 1-0, followed by 2-1, 2-0 and 3-1. In other words, the simplest one-goal victories are followed by the simplest two-goal victories. The precise possibility of any of those scores occurring will obviously vary from match to match. In **Graph 8** I have illustrated how. Like Graph 7, it was produced with data extracted from the last 14 seasons of the Premier and Football Leagues.

If you know how likely it is that a team will win

GRAPH 8

FREQUENCY WITH WHICH TEAMS WON BY SPECIFIC SCORE
(Premier and Football Leagues 1995-96 to 2008-09)

1-0

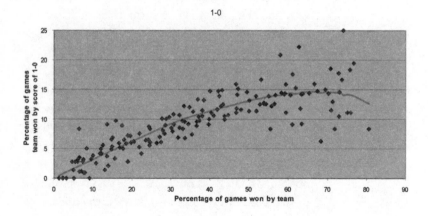

2-0

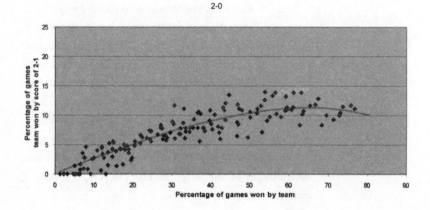

2-1

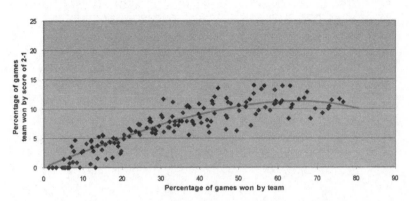

3-1

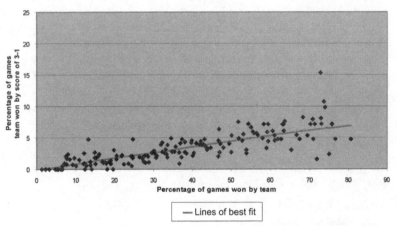

— Lines of best fit

– and you do – you will now be able to work out how likely it is that the team will win 1-0, 2-1, 2-0 or 3-1. A team with a 60 per cent chance of winning, for example, has a 14 per cent chance of winning 1-0, an 11 per cent chance of winning 2-1, an 11 per cent chance of winning 2-0 and a five per cent chance of winning 3-1. Alternatively, a team with only a 40 per cent chance of winning has an 11 per cent chance of winning 1-0, a nine per cent chance of winning 2-1, a seven per cent chance of winning 2-0 and a four per cent chance of winning 3-1.

SELECTED COORDINATES FROM LINES OF BEST FIT ON GRAPH 8				
Percentage of games won by team	Percentage of games team won by score of:			
	1-0	2-1	2-0	3-1
5.0	1.6	1.4	0.5	0.3
10.0	3.2	2.7	1.3	0.8
15.0	4.7	3.9	2.2	1.3
20.0	6.2	5.1	3.1	1.8
25.0	7.7	6.2	3.9	2.2
30.0	9.2	7.3	4.8	2.6
35.0	10.4	8.3	5.8	3.1
40.0	11.4	9.1	6.7	3.6
45.0	12.3	9.8	7.6	4.0
50.0	13.2	10.4	8.6	4.4
55.0	13.8	10.9	9.7	4.9
60.0	14.3	11.2	10.7	5.3
65.0	14.6	11.3	11.8	5.8
70.0	14.6	11.2	12.8	6.2
75.0	14.2	10.8	13.6	6.5
80.0	12.6	10.1	13.6	6.9

Or, at least, it does if the goals expectation for the match is normal. If the number of goals likely to be scored is abnormally low or high, these percentages will vary. In a game in which very few goals are anticipated, for example, the prospect of a 1-0 victory is better than it is in a game in which very many goals are anticipated.

In my opinion, the winning scores that will sometimes be quoted at odds that are too generous include small victories for good teams, particularly in games in which not many goals were foreseen at the outset. Think of it this way: if Manchester United are playing at home to Bolton, which of these two possibilities is more likely to be underestimated – Manchester United winning by a big score or Manchester United winning by a small score?

As well as betting on the score in a match, and the number of goals gained by an individual team,

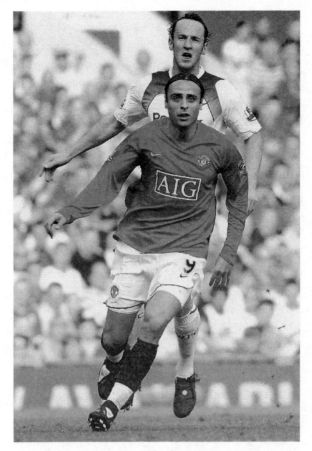

Dimitar Berbatov of Manchester United alarms Bolton

you can also bet on the goal difference between the teams – this is called a handicap bet. Each team is given a handicap. For one team it will be a minus number, for the other it will be a plus number. If one team is given a handicap of -0.5, the other will be given a handicap of +0.5, and so on.

The simplest handicaps are the so-called half-ball handicaps.

If you back a team with a handicap of -0.5, your bet will be successful if the team wins by one or more goals – in other words, so long as it wins the match.

And if it does not? Your bet will be unsuccessful. If you back a team with a handicap of -1.5, your bet will be successful if the team wins by two or more goals. And if it does not? Your bet will be unsuccessful. You get the picture.

In each of these examples, as I am sure you will have realised, your bet being successful means that all bets placed by other people on the other team will be unsuccessful, and vice versa.

You will encounter many other types of handicap. Before placing a handicap bet, always make sure that you have established exactly what your selection has to do for you to be paid out.

You already know how to work out the possibility of a team winning a match – that is to say, beating a handicap of -0.5. In **Graph 9** I have illustrated the relationship between the percentage chance of a team winning a match and the percentage chance of it beating a handicap of -1.5 and -2.5. Once again, the graph was compiled with data from the last 14 seasons of the Premier and Football Leagues.

So now you can work out the percentage chance of a team beating a handicap of -0.5, -1.5 and -2.5 – in other words, winning by one or more goals, two or more goals and three or more goals. You can go on from here to work out the percentage chance of a team winning by exactly one goal and exactly two goals. If, say, there is a 23 per cent chance of a team winning by two or more goals and a nine per cent chance of it winning by three or more goals, there must be an 14 per cent chance of it winning by exactly two goals: 23 - 9 = 14. And so on. The same caveat applies, though, as it does with scores. The figures will vary in games likely to produce either an unusually small or an unusually large number of goals.

GRAPH 9

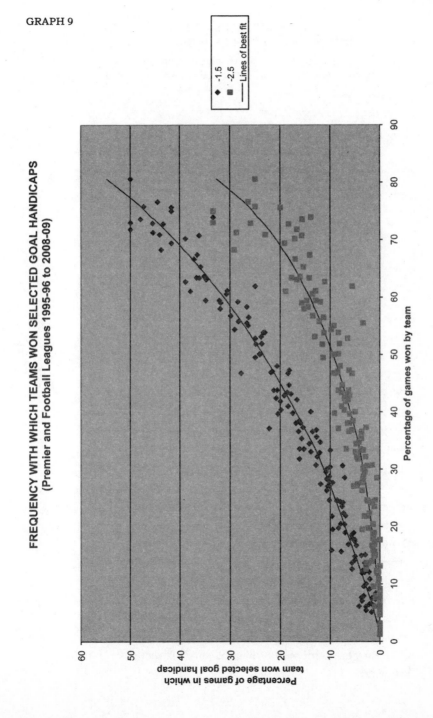

FREQUENCY WITH WHICH TEAMS WON SELECTED GOAL HANDICAPS
(Premier and Football Leagues 1995-96 to 2008-09)

Percentage of games in which team won selected goal handicap

Percentage of games won by team

♦ -1.5
■ -2.5
— Lines of best fit

SELECTED COORDINATES FROM LINES OF BEST FIT ON GRAPH 9		
Percentage of games won by team	Percentage of games in which team won goal handicap of:	
	-1.5	-2.5
5.0	1.1	0.2
10.0	2.9	0.5
15.0	4.9	1.0
20.0	7.0	1.7
25.0	9.1	2.4
30.0	11.3	3.3
35.0	13.9	4.4
40.0	16.9	5.9
45.0	20.0	7.6
50.0	23.4	9.4
55.0	27.1	11.6
60.0	31.3	14.1
65.0	35.8	17.1
70.0	41.0	20.8
75.0	46.8	25.4
80.0	54.0	31.9

You now have all the information you need to be able to evaluate the prospects of any team in any match exceeding, reaching or falling short of a great number of handicaps.

The excited fans interviewed on television at the start of this chapter were really saying what they would like to happen, which may or may not bear any relation to what is likely to happen. You can do much more. You can now estimate, with some accuracy, the percentage chance of any team in any match hitting different numbers of goals, achieving different scores and winning by different margins. In the next chapter, we will turn our attention for a moment away from the teams toward the players of which they are composed. Which players will score? And why?

CHAPTER 6

WHICH PLAYERS WILL GET ON THE SCORESHEET?

THE MOST DIFFICULT SKILL IN FOOTBALL is putting the ball in the back of the net. It is for this reason that attackers command higher fees and bigger salaries than defenders, and it is also why they excite even greater hero worship. Every 12 months the Football Writers' Association in England votes for a Footballer of the Year. None of the last 20 recipients of this award has been a defender.

It is harder to create than to destroy, as television summariser Ruud Gullit said when explaining why he thought Barcelona deserved to beat Chelsea over two legs in the 2009 Champions League semi-final. Back in 1966, brothers Jack and Bobby Charlton won the World Cup with England. Years later, Jack said: "Bobby could play. I stopped other people from playing." Every team needs its Jacks as well as its Bobbys. Nonetheless, those who spend most of their time trying to make things happen will always be more highly valued than those who spend most of their time trying to prevent things from happening.

Any player on the pitch is capable of scoring a goal, however. If you want to bet on scorers, the only thing that should really matter to you is whether a player is more likely to get his name on the sheet than the odds suggest. Over the next few pages we will be

Andres Iniesta celebrates his Champions League goal for Barcelona at Chelsea

investigating two types of goalscorer bet – who will score the first goal of the match and who will score at any time during the match?

First one first. Will this player score the opening goal of the match? You have already done a lot of the work. In Chapter 3 you learnt how to assess the prospects of a team scoring the first goal in a match. All you need to be able to do now is answer one more question. If his team does score the first goal of the match, what are the prospects of the final touch being applied by this player? You can put that another way. You want to know what proportion of the team's goal he can be expected to score.

We need some guidelines. *The OPTA Football Yearbook*, which sadly is no longer published, used to breakdown Premier League goalscorers by position. In the three seasons from 1999-2000 to 2001-2002, it said, 54.5 per cent of Premier League goals were scored by attackers, 32.5 per cent by midfielders and 10.0 per cent by defenders, with the remaining 3.0 per cent being own goals. So that you can find them easily if you are flicking back through this book at a later date, I have reproduced those figures in **Table 4**.

We can use them as a starting point. At that time, nearly all Premier League teams played 4-4-2. We can say that for a typical team playing 4-4-2 just over 27 per cent of goals will be scored by each forward, just over eight per cent by each midfielder and just over two per cent by each defender. The remainder, three per cent, will be own goals – and you should always make allowance for them. For a typical team, each goal is more likely to be scored by an opponent than it is to be scored by any individual defender.

Obviously few teams, if any, are typical. In most strike partnerships, one goal-getter is more prolific than the other. A midfielder who takes free kicks is likely to score more goals than one who does not. A defender who goes forward for set pieces is likely to score more goals than one who stays on the halfway line to guard against counter-attacks.

You have to juggle with the figures. I suggest a three-pronged approach:

1) Look at how many goals players have scored in the past.
2) Use your knowledge of the team's current formation and tactics to judge whether any players are likely to score more or fewer goals in the future.
3) Draw upon your answers to 1) and 2) to compile a list showing the proportion of a team's goals that you expect each player to score.

WHO SCORED THE GOALS?	
(Premier League 1999-2000 to 2001-02)	
Type of players	Percentage of all goals scored
Attackers	54.5
Midfielders	32.5
Defenders	10.0
Opponents (own goals)	3.0

TABLE 4

Remember that there can be a lot of luck involved in goalscoring as well. A midfielder who scores eight goals in one season might score none in the next, but it does not necessarily mean that he was playing better offensively in the first season than he was in the second. He might just have been lucky in the first season and/or unlucky in the second. The difference between a defender blocking a shot and it fizzing past his toe can be minute. The difference between the ball hitting the inside of a post and bouncing in, or hitting the outside of a post and bouncing out, can be minute. And so on, and so on.

In the Introduction, I mentioned tossing a coin. There is a 50 per cent chance of it landing on heads and a 50 per cent chance of it landing on tails. If you toss a coin 38 times – once for each game in a Premier League season – it is exceedingly unlikely that you will get 19 heads and 19 tails. In goalscoring, too, there can be a lot of variation. Be slow to upgrade your expectations of players who, by their standards, have recently been scoring an unusually large number of goals, and be slow to downgrade your expectations of players who, by their standards, have recently been scoring an unusually small number of goals.

Right, suppose you think that player Y can be expected to score 30 per cent of the goals scored by team Z. In other words, you think that each time team Z scores a goal there is a 30 per cent chance of it being scored by player Y. And suppose you think that in a match about to take place there is a 50 per cent chance of team Z scoring the first goal. What is the percentage chance of the first goal being scored by player Y? It is 15 per cent: (30 ÷ 100) x (50 ÷ 100) x 100 = 15. You can use that simple final formula to calculate the percentage chance of any player scoring the first goal in any match.

In theory, you should allow for the possibility of the first goal being an own goal and your player scoring the second goal. Own goals do not count for the purposes of first goalscorer betting. In practice, it does not make much difference. You might want to make an adjustment, though, for the possibility of your player being substituted before the first goal is scored – or, alternatively, starting the match on the bench and being sent on while the score is still 0-0.

As well as quantifying the prospects of player Y scoring the first goal, you will also want to quantify the prospects of him scoring at any time. How do you do this? Consult **Table 5**.

It works in a very similar way to **Table 1** back in Chapter 1. We already know that player Y can be expected to score 30 per cent of team Z's goals, and we will assume that in the match about to take place team Z has a goals expectation of 1.5. Run your finger down the rows on the left-hand side until it reaches 1.5. Now run your finger horizontally across the page until it is immediately underneath the column headed 30. The figure you are pointing at is 36. There is a 36 per cent chance of player Y scoring at least once during the match. Or, at least, there is if he is on the pitch for 90 minutes. You might want to make an adjustment for him being substituted before the final whistle.

You can use **Table 5** to give yourself a pretty good idea of the likelihood of most players scoring in

PERCENTAGE CHANCE OF PLAYER SCORING AT LEAST ONCE DURING A MATCH							
Goals expectation of team:	Percentage of team's goals player is expected to score:						
	5	10	15	20	25	30	35	40
0.5	2	5	7	10	12	14	16	18
0.6	3	6	9	11	14	16	19	21
0.7	3	7	10	13	16	19	22	24
0.8	4	8	11	15	18	21	24	27
0.9	4	9	13	16	20	24	27	30
1.0	5	10	14	18	22	26	30	33
1.1	5	10	15	20	24	28	32	36
1.2	6	11	16	21	26	30	34	38
1.3	6	12	18	23	28	32	37	41
1.4	7	13	19	24	30	34	39	43
1.5	7	14	20	26	31	36	41	45
1.6	8	15	21	27	33	38	43	47
1.7	8	16	23	29	35	40	45	49
1.8	9	16	24	30	36	42	47	51
1.9	9	17	25	32	38	43	49	53
2.0	10	18	26	33	39	45	50	55
2.1	10	19	27	34	41	47	52	57
2.2	10	20	28	36	42	48	54	58
2.3	11	21	29	37	44	50	55	60
2.4	11	21	30	38	45	51	57	62
2.5	12	22	31	39	46	53	58	63

most matches. It will often be lower than you think. Over the last 14 seasons – 1995-1996 to 2008-2009 – Manchester United have scored an average of 2.0 goals per game in the Premier League. Only a very good team will get that many. A player who scored 35 per cent of the goals for a team who averaged 2.0 goals per game could be expected to appear on the scoresheet in 50 per cent of his matches. In other words, even a very prolific striker for a very prolific team might still fail to score in half of his matches.

Some players will, however, be more likely to score than the odds suggest. Which ones will they be? Two types, really. First, players who are simply more likely

TABLE 5

Wayne Bridge scores opening goal of 2007 Carling Cup semi-final for Chelsea

to score on any occasion than most people realise. And secondly, players who are more likely to score on a particular occasion because they will be operating in a more advanced position than they usually do.

Wayne Bridge, then of Chelsea, landed a famous gamble to score the first goal in a 2007 Carling Cup semi-final first leg at Wycombe. He was backed by people who knew that he would be playing on the left wing rather than in his customary position of left back. Remember this, though. If a centre half is asked to stand in at centre forward during an injury crisis, he is more likely to score than he would otherwise have been – but less likely than the regular centre forward. Otherwise he would be playing up front every week. The most difficult skill in football is putting the ball in the back of the net.

CHAPTER 7

WHEN WILL THE GOALS BE SCORED?

IT ONLY TAKES A SECOND TO SCORE A GOAL, Brian Clough used to say. He was right and wrong. Yes, the ball can cross the line in an instant. But usually there has to be a build-up to that moment. And many attacks do not end with a goal. In fact, an overwhelming majority of attacks do not even end with a shot. In the Premier and Football Leagues a goal is scored on average once every 35 minutes – and, remember, there are two teams trying to score that goal.

If goals were distributed uniformly throughout games, as many would be scored in the first half as in the second half. In fact, only 44 per cent of Premier and Football League goals are scored in the first half and 56 per cent are scored in the second half.

What this tells us is that goals become more likely as a game goes on. Why should this be? Arguably it is simply because players try harder to score as the final whistle approaches. With time running out, teams inject ever more urgency into their attempts to score the goals they still need to turn an impending defeat into a draw or an impending draw into a victory.

Graph 10 shows the times at which goals were scored in Premier and Football League games played during the last 12 seasons, 1997-98 to 2008-09. You will see that the number of goals scored increased slowly but steadily almost minute by minute.

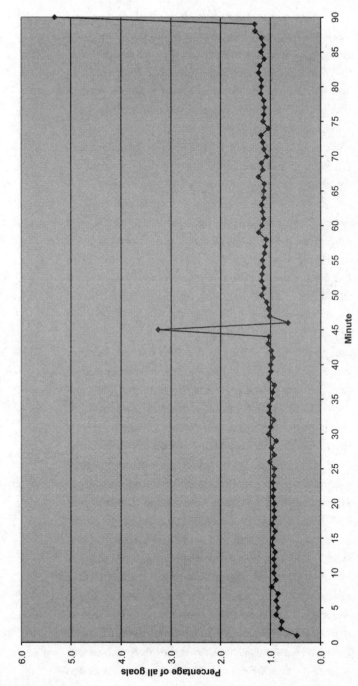

GRAPH 10

WHEN GOALS WERE SCORED
(Premier and Football Leagues 1997-98 to 2008-09)

There were two big jumps, in the 45th minute and in the 90th minute. The reason is that these 'minutes' last longer than any others. At the end of each half, the referee adds stoppage time to compensate for injuries, substitutions, time wasting and so on. In England – though not in some other countries – goals scored in added time at the end of the first half are recorded as being scored in the 45th minute, and goals scored in added time at the end of the second half are recorded as being scored in the 90th minute.

Three times as many goals were recorded as having been scored in the 45th minute as in the 44th minute, and four times as many goals were recorded as having been scored in the 90th minute as in the 89th minute. We can deduce that on average the 45th minute, including stoppage time, lasted about three times as long as the 44th minute and the 90th minute, including stoppage time, lasted about four times as long as the 89th minute. In other words, referees added an average of approximately two minutes stoppage time to the first half and approximately three minutes to the second half.

You might say that the figure for the first half sounds like a lot. To which I would say two things. First, how else do you explain the number of goals scored in the extended 45th minute? And second, be aware that in England the amount of time referees add at the end of the first half is almost never zero.

The referee signals to a fourth official, who holds aloft an electronic board displaying a number of minutes. Even if there have been no injuries or suspensions, and even if there has been no time wasting, English referees almost never feel able to signal a zero. Five hundred and nine Premier League games were televised live during the last three seasons – 2006-07 to 2008-09 – and in only two of them was no stoppage time played at the end of the first half. Crowds therefore howl in angry disbelief during Champions League ties if a continental referee – it happens most often with officials from Germany or Austria – blows his whistle for half time after exactly 45 minutes.

If referees allowed for all interruptions to play – including free kicks, goal kicks, corners, throw ins and so on – games would take much longer to complete. In the Champions League during the last nine seasons – 2000-01 to 2008-09 – the ball was in play for an average of just 56 minutes out of every theoretical 90. In international competitions like the European Championship and World Cup, the figure was similar – if anything, a bit lower. For well over a third of the time that football matches are supposed to be in progress, the ball is actually dead.

The more goals there are likely to be in a match the earlier the first one is likely to arrive. You could have guessed that for yourself. It is easy to overestimate how much earlier, however. **Graph 11** illustrates the relationship between the number of goals in a match and the time of the first goal. Like **Graph 10**, it was compiled with data collected over the last 12 seasons of the Premier and Football Leagues. If you look closely, you will see that in high scoring games an early goal was more likely than it was in low scoring games – but not all that much more likely. Conversely, you will notice that in high scoring games a late start to the scoring was less likely than it was in low scoring games – but not all that much less likely.

In my experience, bookmakers' odds sometimes overestimate the possibility of a late start to the scoring in games they think will be both high scoring and very lopsided. In particular, they overestimate the possibility of the first goal being scored either in

GRAPH 11

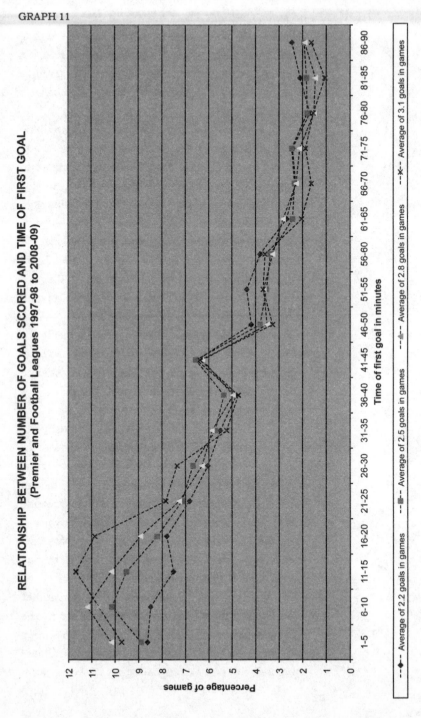

RELATIONSHIP BETWEEN NUMBER OF GOALS SCORED AND TIME OF FIRST GOAL
(Premier and Football Leagues 1997-98 to 2008-09)

the last 15 minutes or the preceding 15 minutes.

It is as though they think an early goal is more likely if one team can be expected to score most of the goals. It isn't. Our estimates for the time of the first goal should vary with our estimates for how many goals will be scored in the whole match, not how many will be scored by any individual team. And as we discovered in Chapter 2, many people overestimate how many goals are likely to be scored in total when a very good team plays a very bad team. It can sometimes take a very long time to score a goal.

CHAPTER 8

WILL IT BE A GAME OF TWO HALVES?

TO UNDERSTAND WHY some half time/full time bets represent value for money, you need to understand how most bettors behave.

A half time/full time bet is a two-part bet. You have to predict what the result will be after both 45 minutes and 90 minutes. A team could be either winning, drawing or losing at half time. And after any of those interval scores, it could be either winning, drawing or losing at full time. So there are always nine possibilities: 3 x 3 = 9.

Imagine that a team likely to finish in the top four of the Premier League is playing at home to a team likely to finish in the bottom four, and imagine that the game is being shown live on television. Which team will most people want to back?

Let me put it this way. Many years ago I was standing with some *Racing Post* colleagues on the trading floor of a spread betting firm before a televised Premier League match between an ordinary Tottenham team and an ordinary Middlesbrough team. Tottenham are a fashionable, London club. Middlesbrough are an unfashionable club from about as far away from London as it is possible to be without leaving England. "Who are they backing?" one of my colleagues shouted to the head of football. "Who do you think they're backing?" was the reply. "Everyone wants to back the favourite."

Like the quote from Jimmy Sirrel at the beginning of this book, it is not quite true, but it is so close to being true that we can forgive the difference. For all practical purposes, it is safe to say that most people want to back the favourite.

It can be the right thing to do. In certain circumstances, you can make money by backing high performing sides, as we shall discover in Chapter 11.

There are different ways of backing the favourite, however. When a very good team is playing at home to a very bad team, the odds quoted for a win by the favourite will be very short indeed. On such occasions, most fun-seeking bettors – who constitute the vast majority of all bettors – will try to find ways of supporting the favourite in other result-related markets that require a more precise prediction but offer, in return, bigger odds. One of the most poplar ways is to back the favourite to be leading after both 45 minutes and 90 minutes.

Obviously, the more likely a team is to be winning at full time the more likely it is to be winning at half time as well. But how much more likely? **Graph 12** tells us. It shows the relationship, for Premier and Football League games played during the last 12 seasons, between the prospect of a team winning a match and the prospect of it achieving three half time/full time results: a half time win followed by a full time win, a half time draw followed by a full time win, and a half time loss followed by a full time win.

You will see that the prospect of a team winning a match has to be as high as 75 per cent for the prospect of it leading at both half time and full time to be as high as 50 per cent. It is rarely, if ever, the overwhelming certainty that many people assume it to be.

We are imagining a game between one of the best

GRAPH 12

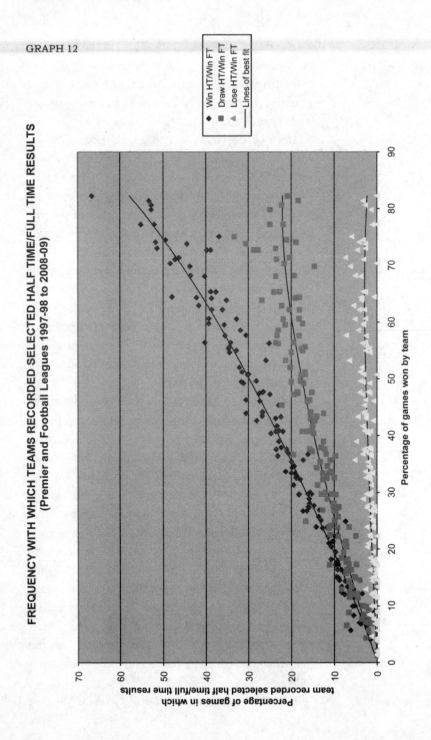

FREQUENCY WITH WHICH TEAMS RECORDED SELECTED HALF TIME/FULL TIME RESULTS
(Premier and Football Leagues 1997-98 to 2008-09)

Percentage of games in which team recorded selected half time/full time results

Percentage of games won by team

- ◆ Win HT/Win FT
- ▓ Draw HT/Win FT
- ▲ Lose HT/Win FT
- — Lines of best fit

SELECTED COORDINATES FROM LINES OF BEST FIT ON GRAPH 12			
Percentage of games won by team	Percentage of games in which team recorded selected half time/full time results		
	Win HT/Win FT	Draw HT/Win FT	Lose HT/Win FT
5	2.4	2.3	0.3
10	5.0	4.3	0.7
15	7.8	6.2	1.0
20	10.7	8.0	1.3
25	13.6	9.8	1.6
30	16.6	11.6	1.8
35	19.7	13.2	2.1
40	23.0	14.7	2.3
45	26.3	16.2	2.5
50	29.8	17.5	2.7
55	33.5	18.7	2.8
60	37.3	19.8	2.9
65	41.3	20.7	3.0
70	45.7	21.4	2.9
75	50.3	21.9	2.8
80	55.4	22.1	2.5

teams in the Premier League and one of the worst. When teams who finished in the top four played at home during the last 12 seasons to teams who finished in the bottom four, there was an 80 per cent chance of a home win and a 55 per cent chance of a home/home double result. Fair odds would therefore have been 1-4 for a home win and around 4-5 for the home team to be leading at both half time and full time.

For such games, the odds bookmakers quote for the home/home double result will vary enormously – perhaps from around 4-6 to around 4-9. None of those odds will represent value for money to you. Some will represent bad value, some will represent very bad value and others will represent appallingly bad value. Many people will take them, however. And because some bookmakers are quoting one half time/full time result at a price that is much, much shorter than it should be, they might quote some of the other possibilities at prices that are bigger than they should be.

The draw/home half time/full time result, for example. You can tell from a line of best fit on **Graph 12** that if the prospect of a team winning is 60 per cent or higher the prospect of it drawing at half time and winning at full time is always greater than 20 per cent. When teams who finished in the top four of the Premier League played at home during the last 12 seasons to teams who finished in the bottom four, the proportion of games in which the draw/home half time/full time result occurred was 22 per cent. Fair odds would therefore have been around 7-2. When a very strong team plays at home to a very weak team, you will sometimes be offered odds for the draw/home half time/full time result that are bigger than they should be. Not always, perhaps not even terribly often, but sometimes.

Many people think of betting as a battle between themselves and a bookmaker. Sun Tzu, the ancient Chinese warlord, said: "If you know the enemy ... you need not fear the result of a hundred battles." When you are betting with a bookmaker, what you really need to understand is not the bookmaker but the other people who are betting with that bookmaker.

Bookmakers sometimes fail to appreciate how likely it is that something will happen. Many more times, in my opinion, they appreciate just how likely it is that something will happen but might still be prepared, in certain situations, to quote odds that are bigger than they should be. They do this quite deliberately. They know from experience what most people will bet on. And because they want to make as much money as possible, they quote odds for those things that are much shorter than they should be, knowing that most people will still take them anyway. And then they might be prepared to quote odds about other things that are bigger than they should be – they do this in a largely forlorn attempt to reduce the anticipated imbalance in their liabilities.

If you know what happens in both halves of a market, you might be able to profit from what happens in both halves of a match.

CHAPTER 9

WHO WILL LIFT THE TROPHY?

IN THE TELEVISION PROGRAMMES 'CRACKER' AND 'WIRE IN THE BLOOD', the police ask a psychologist to tell them what type of person is most likely to have committed a crime. The psychologists employ a technique called offender profiling. The theory behind it is that the person who committed this crime is likely to share distinguishing characteristics with people who have committed similar crimes in the past.

We can employ a comparable technique to help us identify the sort of football team most likely to win a competition. If teams who performed well in a competition in the past exhibited particular characteristics, it seems reasonable to suggest that other teams who share those characteristics might also perform well in the future. In this chapter, we will profile past winners of various domestic and international club competitions: the Premier League, the Football League Championship, League One and League Two, the FA Cup, the Scottish Premier League, the Champions League and the Club World Cup. So let's begin.

PREMIER LEAGUE It takes time to put together a team strong enough to win the Premier League. In recent years, the title has always gone to a team that finished very high in the table the year before.

In six of the last 14 seasons, the Premier League was won by the same team that won it the season before. In six seasons the winner was the team that finished second the season before. And in two seasons the winner was the team that finished third the season before. In other words, none of the winners had finished outside of the top three in the previous season.

You would have to go all the way back to season 1991-92 to find a team that won the top division of English football without having finished in the first three the season before. And where had Howard Wilkinson's Leeds finished at the end of the previous season? Fourth.

In the last few years, the Premier League has been dominated by a so-called Big Four of Arsenal, Chelsea, Liverpool and Manchester United – a quartet of teams with not greatly dissimilar potential. It seems plausible to suggest that the prospect of a team rising from at least slightly outside the top three to win the Premier League might be a bit higher now than it has been for some time – but, at the moment, this is no more than a plausible speculation.

FOOTBALL LEAGUE In each of the statistical examples quoted in this section, the most recent season mentioned was in the period 1995-96 to 2008-09.

The successful teams in the Football League were often those who had narrowly missed out on promotion the season before. You could have largely discounted any survivors from the bottom half of a table. Only four of the 386 non-relegated teams who finished in the bottom half of a division of the Football League went on the following season to win promotion as champions – just one per cent.

A typical relegated team should have been a

TABLE 6

WHERE DID THE TITLE WINNERS COME FROM?
(1995-96 to 2008-09)

Premier League	
Position in previous season	Number of teams who won title in following season
1	6
2	6
3	2
4-17	0
Championship	0

Championship	
Position in previous season	Number of teams who won title in following season
3	2
4	1
5	0
6	0
7	2
8	1
9	1
10	0
11	0
12	0
13	0
14	0
15	0
16	0
17	1
18	0
19	0
20	1
21	0
Premier League	5
League One	0

League One	
Position in previous season	Number of teams who won title in following season
3	0
4	0
5	2
6	1

7	1
8	1
9	0
10	2
11	0
12	1
13	1
14	0
15	0
16	0
17	0
18	0
19	0
20	0
Championship	2
League Two	3

League Two

Position in previous season	Number of teams who won title in following season
4	1
5	1
6	1
7	1
8	1
9	0
10	1
11	1
12	1
13	0
14	1
15	0
16	0
17	0
18	0
19	0
20	0
21	0
22	0
23	0
24	0
League One	3
Conference	2

20-1 shot the following season to win League One or League Two, but only a 7-1 or 8-1 shot to win the Championship. Two of the 43 teams relegated from the Championship to League One (five per cent) won promotion the following season as champions, as did three of the 57 teams (also five per cent) relegated from League One to League Two.

It is widely assumed that the difference in standard between the Premier League and Championship is greater than the difference between the Championship and League One or League One and League Two. And the fortunes of relegated clubs confirm that this is so.

Five of the 43 teams relegated from the Premier League returned the following season as winners of the Championship – between 11 and 12 per cent. Remember, though, these teams would almost always have been highly fancied in betting markets.

It is possible that the gulf in class between the Premier League and Championship is extensive, but not quite as extensive as many people allow themselves to surmise. The average finishing position of teams relegated from the Premier League in their first season in the Championship was eighth. If you told a representative group of English football followers that a typical team relegated from the Premier League would finish outside of the play-off places in the Championship, they probably would not believe you – but you would be right and they would be wrong.

In fact, the manager of a team relegated from the Premier League is more likely to be out of his job before the end of the following season than he is to finish it as winner of the Championship. The two possibilities are not unconnected, of course. A team relegated from the Championship will be optimistic

The FA Cup is usually won by a top team: Chelsea hoisted the trophy in 2009

– often unrealistically optimistic – of an immediate return to the Premier League. And if it begins to look as though this will not happen, the manager can be out on his ear. Twenty-two of the 43 clubs newly relegated from the Premier League parted company with their manager during their first season in the Championship – more than half.

Promoted teams never won the Championship, but did sometimes claim titles in Leagues One and Two.

We go back now to the teams in each division who had finished in the top half of that division the season before. The closer to the top they finished the more likely they were to follow up with promotion as champions. A typical team finishing in one of the five highest non-promotion places should have been a 13-1 shot to do better in the following season and win promotion as champions. Between seven and eight per cent of such teams lifted a title – 16 out of 213.

FA CUP Alan Hansen, eight times a league winner and two times an FA Cup winner as a player with Liverpool, once said that the best team wins the league and the luckiest team wins the FA Cup. Nowadays, exceptionally good teams tend to win the FA Cup as well – even though it is not their highest priority and they often rest star players, particularly in the early rounds.

In 13 of the 14 years between 1996 and 2009, the winner of the FA Cup was Arsenal, Chelsea, Liverpool or Manchester United. And at least one of those four teams featured in the final in 20 of the 22 years between 1988 and 2009.

WHERE DID THE FA CUP WINNERS COME FROM? (1985 to 2009)	
Position in Premier League at start of FA Cup third round	Number of teams who won FA Cup
1	3
2	4
3	3
4	3
5	2
6	3
7	1
8	2
9	2
10	0
11	0
12	0
13	0
14	0
15	1
16	0
17	0
18	0
19	0
20	1
21	0
22	0

TABLE 7

Premier League teams enter the FA Cup in the third round, which is usually played over the first weekend in January. To win the FA Cup, a Premier League team has to overcome six opponents. If you look at **Table 7**, you will see that the higher a team sat in the top division of English football on the morning of third round day the more likely it was to lift the FA Cup. Table 7 covers the quarter-century from 1985 to 2009. Of the 75 teams positioned between first and third in the top division, ten won the FA Cup – 13 per cent. Of the 75 teams positioned between fourth and sixth in the top division, eight won the FA Cup – 11 per cent. Of the 75 teams positioned between seventh and ninth in the top division, five won the FA Cup – seven per cent.

Only two of the 290 teams positioned lower than ninth in the top division won the FA Cup – just half a per cent. And not once in the entire quarter century did a team from outside of the top division get to lift the FA Cup. Is there anyone out there who still believes that the famous old tournament, in the words of one of its many clichés, is a great leveller?

SCOTTISH PREMIER LEAGUE **Celtic or Rangers.**

CHAMPIONS LEAGUE **The unromantic truth about modern football at the highest level is that the richest clubs can afford to buy the best players and win most of the honours.**

The richest national leagues in Europe are those of England, Spain and Italy, followed by Germany and France – at the moment, pretty much in that order. Those five countries have the most powerful economies in western Europe.

In the 17 years since the European Cup evolved into the Champions League the competition has been won five times by clubs from Spain, four times by clubs from Italy, three times by clubs from England, twice by clubs from Germany and once by a club from France. On the other two occasions the trophy went to a club from Holland and a club from Portugal.

If you want to find the winners of the Champions League, you should probably search among the representatives of the biggest and wealthiest countries in western Europe.

In recent years, English clubs have performed particularly well – featuring in each of the five finals from 2005 to 2009, though winning only two of them.

England's prominence has irked the French president of Uefa, Michel Platini. If he studied **Table 8**, he might calm down. It shows the countries represented in the final of the European Cup and Champions League in each of the 54 years since the competition began.

You will see that the history of Europe's premier club competition is one of countries enjoying little clusters of success, which end as surely as they begin – first there was Spain, followed by Portugal, Italy, Holland, Germany and England, then Italy again, Spain again and, finally, England again. England's present pre-eminence will pass – though probably only to Spain or Italy.

CLUB WORLD CUP The champions of South America can be underestimated in contests with the champions of Europe.

The best teams from the two continents have met almost every year for nearly half a century. The World Club Championship, as it was called, brought together the champions of Europe and the champions of South America, the winners of the

Brazilian club Internacional celebrate winning the 2006 Club World Cup in Japan after beating Barcelona 2-1

Copa Libertadores. It was a two-legged home and away contest between 1960 and 1980, when it was reduced to a single-legged contest played annually in Japan.

In 2005 the competition was renamed the Club World Cup and expanded to include the champions of each of Fifa's six continental regions – Africa, Asia, Central and North America, and Oceania, as well as Europe and South America. And a local guest as well. From 2005 to 2008 the tournament was played in Japan but in 2009 it will move to the United Arab Emirates. Each of the four Club World Cup finals in Japan has been contested between the champions of Europe and the champions of South America.

EUROPEAN CUP AND CHAMPIONS LEAGUE FINALISTS BY COUNTRY					
Year	Italy	Spain	England	Germany	Portugal	Holland
1956		1				
1957	1	1				
1958	1	1				
1959		1				
1960		1		1		
1961		1			1	
1962		1			1	
1963	1				1	
1964	1	1				
1965	1				1	
1966		1				
1967	1					
1968			1		1	
1969	1					1
1970						1
1971						1
1972	1					1
1973	1					1
1974		1		1		
1975			1	1		
1976				1		
1977			1	1		
1978			1			
1979			1			
1980			1	1		
1981		1	1			
1982			1	1		
1983	1			1		
1984	1		1			
1985	1		1			
1986		1				
1987				1	1	
1988					1	1
1989	1					
1990	1				1	
1991						
1992	1	1				
1993	1					
1994	1	1				

EUROPEAN CUP AND CHAMPIONS LEAGUE FINALISTS BY COUNTRY							
Year	France	Romania	Scotland	Yugoslavia	Greece	Belgium	Sweden
1956	1						
1957							
1958	1						
1959							
1960							
1961							
1962							
1963							
1964							
1965							
1966				1			
1967			1				
1968							
1969							
1970			1				
1971					1		
1972							
1973							
1974							
1975							
1976	1						
1977							
1978						1	
1979							1
1980							
1981							
1982							
1983							
1984							
1985							
1986		1					
1987							
1988		1					
1989							
1990							
1991	1			1			
1992							
1993							
1994	1						

EUROPEAN CUP AND CHAMPIONS LEAGUE FINALISTS BY COUNTRY						
Year	Italy	Spain	England	Germany	Portugal	Holland
1995	1					
1996	1					1
1997	1					1
1998	1	1				
1999			1	1		
2000		2				
2001		1		1		
2002		1		1		
2003	2					
2004					1	
2005	1		1			
2006		1	1			
2007	1		1			
2008			2			
2009		1	1			
All	25	21	17	13	9	8

If we accept these various arrangements as developments of the same competition, we can say that 47 finals have pitted the champions of Europe against the champions of South America. Twenty-three times the Europeans have won and 24 times the South Americans have won. Over a fairly extended period of time, therefore, the champions of South America have performed at a level that has been at least comparable to the champions of Europe. The results at 90 minute in the one-off games played since 1980 in Japan have been 12 victories for South America, eight draws and nine victories for Europe.

Europeans say they take the competition less seriously than the South Americans. The South Americans say their teams are simply better than arrogant Europeans will acknowledge. Nowadays, the top players from South America all come to Europe. However, those representing the champion team of South America in the Club World Cup will

EUROPEAN CUP AND CHAMPIONS LEAGUE FINALISTS BY COUNTRY							
Year	France	Romania	Scotland	Yugoslavia	Greece	Belgium	Sweden
1995							
1996							
1997							
1998							
1999							
2000							
2001							
2002							
2003							
2004							
2005	1						
2006							
2007							
2008							
2009							
All	6	2	2	2	1	1	1

TABLE 8

be hoping to become the next young starlets to land a big money move to Barcelona, Real Madrid, Inter, Juventus or Milan.

Whatever the reason, the champions of South America have for a long time at least equalled the champions of Europe. Yet in outright and match betting markets they are almost always regarded as significantly inferior.

In 'Cracker' and "Wire in the Blood', the psychologist has only to describe the person most likely to have committed a crime. You have to do a bit more. You have to evaluate the prospects of a football team winning a competition. And then you have to hope that somebody else produces an evaluation that is both different and less accurate. The skill ultimately required of odds profilers, as opposed to offender profilers, is always the same: being able to identify outcomes that are more likely than somebody else understands.

CHAPTER 10

WHY MANAGERS GET THE SACK

MANAGERS DO NOT LOSE THEIR JOBS BECAUSE OF BAD RESULTS. They lose their jobs because of unexpectedly bad results. The extra word is all-important. Remember it if you bet in so-called sack race markets – perhaps the next manager to go, or which managers will or will not still be in their post at the end of a season. Focus not so much on bad teams as on ordinary or good teams who could go through a bad patch, if only a very brief one.

Consider this. Managers of clubs newly promoted to the Premier League are always less likely to lose their jobs than managers of clubs longer established in the Premier League, even though many of them get relegated straight back to the Championship. The reason is that for many of them relegation was always acknowledged by the club's owners as a strong possibility. During the last 12 seasons, only five of the 36 clubs newly promoted to the Premier League parted company with their manager – just 14 per cent.

The casualty rate at other Premier League clubs was almost twice as high – 24 per cent. The most telling statistic about those other Premier League clubs is that when they parted company with their manager they were, on average, five places lower in the table than they had been at the end of the previous season.

Tony Adams was promoted to manager of Portsmouth

When the axe does fall, it can fall quickly. In eight of the last 12 seasons at least one Premier League manager had gone before the end of September and in none of those 12 seasons did all 20 managers survive beyond the end of November.

As soon as a manager clears his desk, bets will be taken on who will be sitting at it next. The terms of these bets will usually refer to the next 'permanent' manger of a club but, you should be aware, interpretations of what is meant by 'permanent' can differ from bookmaker to bookmaker.

The possibility that is sometimes underestimated is an internal promotion. When Harry Redknapp left Portsmouth in October 2008 to become manager of Tottenham, his successor was his assistant, Tony Adams. And when Adams was sacked in February

2009 after a run of very bad results, his replacement was youth team coach Paul Hart – albeit, at the time, only on a short term contract until the end of the season. When Roy Keane resigned as manager of Sunderland in December 2008, his successor was first team coach Ricky Sbragia.

There are three reasons why you might sometimes be offered odds that underestimate the possibility of an internal promotion. First, backroom staff will usually have a low public profile. Second, the owners of a club might initially want to appoint somebody from outside but the people on their wish list either might not want the job or might not be available, especially if a season is in progress.

And third, an internal candidate might be asked to stand in as temporary manager while the owners conduct a recruitment process, and this will give him an opportunity to impress. If he strings together two or three promising results, a clamour will arise among supporters and the media for him to be given the job of full time manager – even though nobody on the outside could possibly know whether his initial success was attributable to judgement or luck. What matters to you, though, is what happens, not whether it always happens for well thought-out reasons. At the start of the 2009-10 season, 19 of the 92 clubs in the Premier and Football Leagues had a coach who had been promoted from within – 21 per cent.

CHAPTER 11

WHAT SORT OF TEAMS SHOULD YOU BET?

YOU CAN MAKE MONEY YEAR AFTER YEAR by betting on the results of football matches. The way to do it is to back good teams and oppose bad teams. The catch – after such a statement, you would be expecting a catch – is that it is much harder than you might think to distinguish between the two.

If you had backed Manchester United to win in every Premier League game they played, you would have made a profit in each of the last five seasons. Throughout this time, Manchester United were either the best or one of the best teams in England.

If you had backed Chelsea, you would have made a profit in four of the last five seasons. If you had followed other members of the Big Four, however, you would have fared less well – losing in three out of five seasons with Liverpool, and also losing in three out of five seasons with Arsenal.

The reason Manchester United and Chelsea would have rewarded their followers is not just that they were very good teams but also that they achieved even better results than most people had anticipated from them. And that is the key. The profitable teams are those who do unexpectedly well (if you are backing them) or unexpectedly badly (if you are opposing them).

Let's go through this step by step. Each year, some teams show a profit for level stakes backers while others show a loss. Is there a way of distinguishing between the former and the latter? As it happens, there is.

If we think of the 92 teams in the Premier and Football Leagues as being a separate entity each season, we can say that over the last five seasons 460 different teams have played in the Premier and Football Leagues. And 198 of them showed a profit – 43 per cent. Overwhelmingly, the teams who made a profit were those who finished near the top of their table and the teams who made a loss were those who finished near the bottom of their table.

The point is illustrated vividly in **Graph 13**. It shows the profit or loss that would have accrued over the last five seasons – 2004-05 to 2008-09 – to consistent backers of teams who finished in different positions in the Premier League and the three divisions of the Football League.

If you had backed every team that finished in the top ten in the Premier League to win in every game, you would have made a profit of five per cent on your turnover. If you had backed every team that finished in the top ten in each division of the Football League, you would have made a profit of nine per cent on your turnover. And if you had backed every team that finished lower than tenth in the Premier League and each division of the Football League you would have made a loss equivalent to 14 per cent of your turnover.

The figures quoted above were calculated from the best prices available with bookmakers featured in the odds comparison table published on the morning of the match in the *Racing Post*. It goes without saying – but is always worth saying – that you should bet at

**RELATIONSHIP BETWEEN LEAGUE POSITION OF TEAMS AND THEIR PROFITABILITY FOR BACKERS
(2004-05 to 2008-09)**

PREMIER LEAGUE

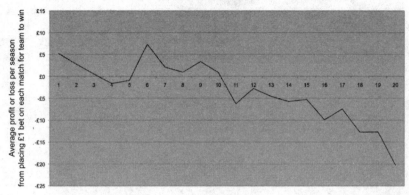

Finishing position of team

FOOTBALL LEAGUE

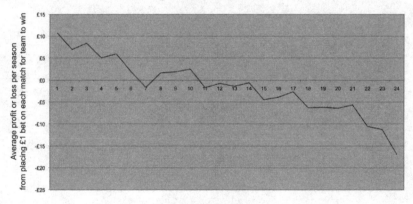

Finishing position of team

GRAPH 13

all times at the best available odds. It is surprising how many people don't. And nowadays there is no excuse. Internet odds comparison sites include most of the markets for which there is not space in the *Racing Post*. If you always bet at the best available odds, you will always obtain the best potential returns.

But if anybody is beginning to think that winning

COORDINATES FOR LINES OF BEST FIT ON GRAPH 13	
Premier League	
Finishing position of team	Average profit or loss per season from placing £1 bet on each match for team to win
1	5.21
2	2.80
3	0.56
4	-1.62
5	-0.89
6	7.33
7	2.14
8	0.95
9	3.38
10	0.92
11	-6.24
12	-2.75
13	-4.56
14	-5.72
15	-5.23
16	-9.94
17	-7.50
18	-12.75
19	-12.70
20	-20.23
Football League	
Finishing position of team	Average profit or loss per season from placing £1 bet on each match for team to win
1	10.74
2	6.95
3	8.38
4	5.05
5	5.94
6	1.94
7	-1.63
8	1.64
9	1.87
10	2.50
11	-1.71

Football League	
Finishing position of team	Average profit or loss per season from placing £1 bet on each match for team to win
12	-0.76
13	-1.40
14	-0.60
15	-4.52
16	-3.93
17	-2.69
18	-6.35
19	-6.22
20	-6.46
21	-5.70
22	-10.54
23	-11.28
24	-16.89

money by betting on football matches is easy – and, hopefully, after reading the preceding chapters, nobody is – well, they will need to think again. Most punters already back teams who are perceived to be good and oppose teams who are perceived to be bad. Most of them lose more money than they win. And that should encourage us to stop and reflect. It is much, much harder than most people are prepared to accept to identify in advance teams who are going to do well and teams who are going to do badly.

The ante-post betting markets effectively express a consensus of everybody's individual opinion. If you had selected the top ten teams in the ante-post betting markets for the Premier League and each division of the Football League and backed them to win in every game, you would have made a big loss. If you had chosen teams who finished in the top ten the season before, you would also have made a big loss. If you had backed all newly promoted teams, you would have incurred another big loss. And if you had backed all recently relegated teams, you would have suffered yet another big loss.

The teams who generate profits are those who perform differently from how most people had assumed they would. In **Table 9**, I have listed the ten largest profits posted in individual seasons. You will see lots of humdrum names – if you will excuse that expression in this particular context – like Stockport, Hartlepool, Luton, Blackpool, Hereford, Rochdale and Blackburn. And that should give us a clue.

You can make money from match betting year after year by backing good teams and opposing bad ones. The good and bad teams, however, are not always the ones that most people think they will be. And it is those who do unexpectedly well or badly who can be really profitable to follow.

Which brings us back to one of the points I was making in the Introduction. After reading every chapter since then, you should now be in a better position to discern the true abilities of teams and

TABLE 9

	TEN HIGHEST PROFITS IN AN INDIVIDUAL SEASON OBTAINED BY PLACING £1 BET IN EACH MATCH FOR TEAM TO WIN (Premier and Football Leagues 2004-05 to 2008-09)			
	Team	Division	Season	Profit in £
1	Stockport	League Two	2007-08	20.04
2	Blackburn	Premier League	2005-06	19.65
3	Millwall	League One	2007-08	18.31
4	Hartlepool	League Two	2006-07	18.19
5	Luton	League One	2004-05	17.24
6	Blackpool	League One	2006-07	17.22
7	Scunthorpe	League One	2006-07	17.05
8	Hereford	League Two	2007-08	16.85
9	Rochdale	League Two	2007-08	16.78
10	Tranmere	League One	2008-09	16.22

determine whether other people are underestimating them or overestimating them. It will not be easy, but it should be less difficult than it might otherwise have been. For those who can acquire the necessary skills, there are profits to be made by betting on the goals that are scored in football matches. And – as we shall discover in the second half of this book – a lot more besides.

SECTION 2

CORNERS AND BOOKINGS

CHAPTER 12

THE GAMES TEAMS PLAY

THE DIFFERENCE BETWEEN A GOOD TEAM AND A BAD TEAM is simply that the good team is more effective than the bad team in everything that it does. It wins the ball back more quickly, and then it gives the ball away more slowly. A good team will therefore have more possession than a bad team. But it will also use that possession more efficiently.

For every minute that it has the ball, it will spend longer in the opposition half. For every minute that it spends in the opposition half, it will have more shots. Of all its shots, a higher proportion will be on target. And of all its shots on target, a higher proportion will end up in the back of the net.

In every way, good teams are more productive than bad teams. The most successful team in the Premier League in the seven seasons from 2002-03 to 2008-09 was Manchester United, who won the title four times and never finished outside of the top four. In the Premier League games in which they participated during those seven seasons, Manchester United were responsible for 57 per cent of possession, 62 per cent of all shots, 65 per cent of all shots on target and 71 per cent of all goals.

We can say two things. The first is that they did more attacking than their opponents. It stands to reason as they had possession of the ball for longer. And the second thing we can say is that the attacking they did was more purposeful. With 57 per cent of the possession, they scored 71 per cent of the goals.

In Chapter 7 we discovered that at the highest levels of football the ball is in play for roughly 56 minutes in every match. We can therefore surmise that in their games Manchester United were in possession for an average of 32 minutes and their opponents for an average of 24 minutes: $57 \div 100 \times 56 = 32$, and $(100 - 57) \div 100 \times 56 = 24$. On average, Manchester United scored 1.90 goals per game and conceded 0.75 goals per game. We can therefore speculate that on average it took Manchester United just 17 minutes of possession to score a goal and their opponents as many as 32 minutes: $32 \div 1.90 = 17$, and $24 \div 0.75 = 32$. In other words, the length of time with the ball that Manchester United required in order to score a goal was little more than half the length of time required by their opponents.

We need to understand the difference between good and bad teams if we want to understand all of the other things beside goals that can happen in football matches. For betting purposes at the moment, those other things are usually corners and bookings. In theory, of course, it would be possible to bet on many other things as well – free kicks, throw ins, goal kicks, offsides and so on – and, in practice, one or two bookmakers are starting to do so.

If you visit an odds comparison site before a televised football match you will be able to click through the odds bookmakers are quoting in upwards of 80 markets. It sounds like a lot, and it is. Almost all of those markets, however, relate to just three of the things that could happen: goals, corners and bookings. And in almost all of those markets you are really being asked to answer just one of two questions, albeit phrased in a great variety of different ways.

How many will there be? And how will they be split between the teams?

In the first part of this book we learnt how to answer those questions when they relate to goals. In the second part we will learn how to answer them when they relate to corners or bookings. It is satisfying to feel that you understand the internal dynamics of a football match. As Sir Bobby Robson, who was then England manager, once said to Charles Hughes, who was then the Football Association's Director of Coaching and Education: "It is because of all the other things that happen in between ... that goals are produced." And it can be profitable, too. In my experience, you are more likely to be offered good bets in corner-related or bookings-related markets than you are in goal-related markets.

There are two reasons. The first is that you can still have the psychological impulses of thrill-of-the-ride bettors working in your favour, because they are still capable in certain circumstances of distorting the odds to your advantage. And you have something else going for you, too.

Bookmakers spend longer trying to work out precisely what the odds should be in primary markets than they do in secondary markets – for the simple reason that they will take much more money on them and will therefore be exposing themselves to a greater risk in return for what they hope will be a greater reward. Before placing which of these two bets would you, as a private person, exercise the greatest care: a bet on which you were going to stake £1,000 or a bet on which you were going to stake £1? The question answers itself. And the answer is exactly the same for bookmakers. Some odds compilers sometimes do not understand quite as accurately what the odds should be in corner or

bookings markets as they do in goal markets. And
with that encouragement, let us move on.

CHAPTER 13

HOW MANY CORNERS WILL BE TAKEN?

IN THIS CHAPTER, we will learn how to work out the percentage chance of different numbers of corners being taken in a match. We will do this in two steps. The first step is to calculate a corners expectation for the match. The second step is to convert that corners expectation into a percentage chance of the total being, say, less than 11, exactly 11, more than 11, or whatever.

By now, you will understand very well what is meant by a phrase like corners expectation. We are asking ourselves this question: if these two teams played each other at this venue a great number of times, how many corners would be taken on average? The answer is our corners expectation.

And what might it be? To calculate a corners expectation for a match, we need to be able to answer two more questions that will become increasingly familiar during the remainder of this book. The first question is: what usually happens in this sort of match? And the second question is: should we anticipate anything unusual from these two teams?

The first question is normally fairly easy to answer. In most seasons, the average number of corners taken in matches is around 11.1 in the Premier League and Football League, 10.6 in the Scottish Premier

Frank Lampard prepares to flight a corner for Chelsea

League, 10.5 in the Bundesliga, 10.3 in Serie A, 10.0 in La Liga and 9.6 in Le Championnat. It is approximately 9.9 in the Champions League.

You will notice that corners tend to occur more frequently in England than they do elsewhere in Europe. Jose Mourinho, formerly manager of Chelsea, once said: "How many countries can you think of where a corner kick is treated with the same applause as a goal? One. It only happens in England. This is the only place where a corner kick is as good as a goal for the fans. And what is the best way to get a corner? Just kicking the ball into the box and pressing the second ball."

He was exaggerating his point to make his point, no doubt, but he does have a point. The very best teams in England all have different styles, but in their own ways they are now as proficient technically and tactically as their counterparts in Spain, Italy and elsewhere, as has been evidenced in recent years by their achievements in the Champions League. In fact, it could be argued that over the decades none of the English clubs that has won the European Cup or Champions League has done so by playing what would be called traditional English football.

Elsewhere in the Premier League and Football League, however, there are still many other teams who rely more heavily on the traditional English call to blood and thunder – or, as it sometimes seems to translate in practice, thud and blunder. One consequence is that the ball ricochets out of play more often.

The second question can be harder to answer. We might know how many corners are usually taken in this sort of match – but should we be anticipating anything unusual from these particular teams?

We find out by employing methods similar to the ones that were employed in Section 1. We can get an idea of how many corners will be taken in a team's future games if we can identify how many corners were taken in its past games. I would suggest that you try to establish how many corners have been taken in a team's games over a period equivalent to roughly a whole season. The optimum number of games, I have found by testing different possibilities, is the last 32, but in most competitions in most countries the last 32 games is not far from being a whole season.

Attach more importance overall to recent fixtures than distant ones. Discount any dissimilarities between home games and away games – unless a team has a well-established pattern that has been evident over several seasons of becoming involved in vastly different corner counts at one venue than another.

Constantly be on the lookout for rare, freak occurrences that might dramatically distort the averages you are computing. Imagine, say, a Premier League team that over the equivalent of a whole season has played 38 games in which there were 436 corners. The average number of corners taken in those games was 11.5. Imagine now that you are scrutinising individual matches and you discover that in one match the total number of corners taken was an extraordinarily high 25. If you ignore the outlier, as statisticians would call it, you will find that the average number of corners taken in the other 37 games was a perfectly ordinary 11.1.

So, now you know how many corners are usually taken in this sort of match and you also know how many corners have usually been taken in the past in the games played by these two teams. How many corners should you expect to be taken today when these two teams play each other?

Generally speaking, teams who have been involved in abnormally high corner counts in the past tend to become involved in abnormally high corner counts in the future as well – but in future the corner counts tend to be less abnormally high than they were in the past. And, likewise, teams who have been involved in abnormally low corner counts in the past tend to become involved in abnormally low corner counts in the future as well – but in future the corner counts tend to be less abnormally low than they were in the past.

You will not be surprised to hear that there are many random factors that can influence the number of corners taken in matches. Indeed, I have intimated as much already. When calculating a corners expectation for a match, I have found, the best results are obtained by giving 58 per cent of the weight in your calculation to what usually happens in that sort of match and 42 per cent to what usually happens in matches of the two teams. We can express that formulaically as follows:

$$C_{AB} = (C_D \times 58 \div 100) +$$
$$(C_A \times C_B \div C_D \times 42 \div 100)$$

In this formula: C_{AB} is the corners expectation for a match about to be played between team A and team B; C_D is the average number of corners taken in matches played in that competition; C_A is the average number of corners taken in matches played in that competition by team A; and C_B is the average number of corners taken in matches played in that competition by team B.

Let's put some flesh on the bones of that formula. Let's imagine a Premier League match about to be played between competitors that we will call team A and team B. On this occasion, we will say, $C_D = 11.1$, $C_A = 11.2$ and $C_B = 11.5$. Our corners expectation for the match therefore becomes:

$$C_{AB} = (11.1 \times 58 \div 100) +$$
$$(11.2 \times 11.5 \div 11.1 \times 42 \div 100)$$
$$= 11.3$$

And how do we convert this corners expectation into the percentage chance of different numbers of corners being taken? Look at **Graph 14**. It shows the relationship in the Premier League during the last 12 seasons between the average number of corners taken in a team's games and the percentage of that team's games in which the number of corners taken was 0-8, 0-9 and so on. We can put that another way: it shows the relationship between the

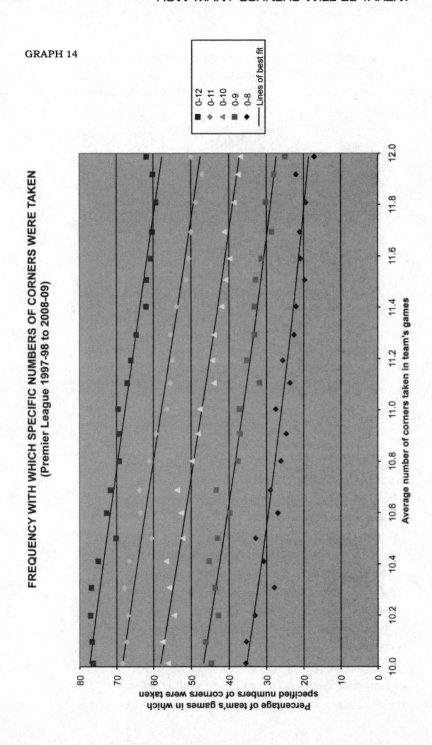

GRAPH 14

FREQUENCY WITH WHICH SPECIFIC NUMBERS OF CORNERS WERE TAKEN
(Premier League 1997-98 to 2008-09)

Percentage of team's games in which specified numbers of corners were taken

Average number of corners taken in team's games

- 0-12
- 0-11
- 0-10
- 0-9
- 0-8
— Lines of best fit

COORDINATES FOR LINES OF BEST FIT ON GRAPH 14					
Average number of corners taken in team's games	Percentage of team's games in which specified numbers of corners were taken:				
	0-8	0-9	0-10	0-11	0-12
10.0	35.4	46.9	58.3	68.6	77.4
10.1	34.4	45.8	57.1	67.5	76.4
10.2	33.3	44.7	56.0	66.5	75.5
10.3	32.4	43.6	54.9	65.4	74.6
10.4	31.4	42.5	53.8	64.3	73.6
10.5	30.4	41.4	52.6	63.3	72.6
10.6	29.5	40.4	51.5	62.2	71.7
10.7	28.6	39.3	50.4	61.1	70.7
10.8	27.7	38.3	49.3	60.0	69.7
10.9	26.8	37.3	48.2	59.0	68.7
11.0	26.0	36.3	47.2	57.9	67.7
11.1	25.1	35.3	46.1	56.8	66.7
11.2	24.3	34.3	45.1	55.7	65.7
11.3	23.5	33.4	44.0	54.7	64.7
11.4	22.8	32.4	43.0	53.6	63.7
11.5	22.0	31.5	42.0	52.6	62.6
11.6	21.3	30.6	40.9	51.5	61.6
11.7	20.6	29.7	40.0	50.5	60.6
11.8	19.9	28.9	39.0	49.4	59.6
11.9	19.2	28.0	38.0	48.4	58.6
12.0	18.5	27.2	37.0	47.4	57.5

corners expectation for a match and the percentage chance of the actual total being no higher than eight, no higher than nine, and so on.

For our imaginary Premier League game between team A and team B, our corners expectation is 11.3. The lines of best fit on Graph 14 – which, by the way, can also be trusted for matches in other competitions in England and elsewhere – tell us the following: there is a 23.5 chance of 0-8 corners being taken, a 33.4 per cent chance of 0-9, a 44.0 per cent chance of 0-10, a 54.7 per cent chance of 0-11 and a 64.7 per cent chance of 0-12. We can deduce other things as well. If there is a 54.7 per cent chance of 0-11 corners and a 64.7 per cent chance of 0-12 corners, it follows that there must be a 10.0 per cent chance of exactly 11 corners (64.7 - 54.7 = 10.0). And if there is a 54.7 per cent chance of 0-11 corners being taken, it also follows that there must be a 45.3 per cent chance of 12 or more corners being taken (100 - 54.7 = 45.3).

We can use Graph 14 to help us determine the prospects of many different numbers of corners being taken in many different games. And that flexibility is vital, because bookmakers offer many different over/under lines and over/middle/under bands for total corner markets.

Where are you most likely to find odds that are bigger than they should be? Before addressing that question directly, it is worth mentioning that corners bets are settled on the number taken, which is not always exactly the same as the number awarded. Suppose nine corners have been taken in a match that is entering the last few moments of added time at the end of the second half. The ball bounces off a defender and goes behind the goal line. The referee gestures toward the corner flag. Before the kick can be taken, however, the referee whistles for full time. Bets will be settled on the nine corners taken, ignoring the tenth that was awarded but never taken.

For much more important reasons – which, by now, will be very familiar to you – it is bets on comparatively small numbers of corners that are most likely to represent value for money. You will be offered overly high odds about low totals for all sorts of games, but particularly, in my experience, for games in which a very good team is playing at home to a very bad team. Quite rightly, most bettors think the hosts are likely to do lots of attacking and force lots of corners. Quite wrongly, they forget that the visitors are likely to do very little attacking and force very few corners. Overall, the number of corners taken in such matches is not excessively high. In the next chapter, we will discuss how the corners taken in a match are likely to be dispersed between the teams.

CHAPTER 14

WHICH TEAM WILL TAKE MOST CORNERS?

ONE OF THE DIFFERENCES between a good team and a bad team, we learnt in Chapter 12, is that it attacks more effectively. If you understand this simple fact, you will be able to make sense of much that happens during football matches. And that will help you when you bet on some of the by-products of attacking play – for example, how corners will be split between teams in markets such as corner handicaps.

Let's recap what we learnt in Chapter 12.

A good team will have the ball for longer than a bad team. For each minute that it has the ball, it will spend longer in the opposition half. For each minute that it spends in the opposition half, it will have more shots. Of all its shots, a higher proportion will be on target. And of all its shots on target, a higher proportion will end up in the back of the net. The key point to hold on to here is that a good team will have to do less attacking to score a goal than a bad team.

Now let's move on to thinking about corners.

In Premier League games played during the last 12 seasons, home teams scored 58 per cent of all goals. We can say that in a game between two teams of equal ability the one enjoying ground advantage should be expected to score 58 per cent of the goals. The home team is not better than the away team, nor is its attacking play more effective. The reason it is the more likely to win the match is simply that it derives a benefit from playing in its own stadium. In such games, logic suggests that the home team should be expected to take around 58 per cent of the corners. In practice, it will normally take around 57 per cent of the corners, but that is only a very small discrepancy and is neither here nor there.

Now let's imagine a game in which both teams can be expected to score the same number of goals. In other words, a game in which the home team is no more or less likely to win than the away team. What have we got here? What we have not got is a home team that is as good as the away team. It is worse, but its inferiority is compensated for by the advantage it gains from playing on its own ground. In short, the home team will have to do more attacking than the away team to score the same number of goals. And for this reason it should be expected to accumulate more corners. It might sound strange to suggest that a team could be only joint favourite to score most goals but outright favourite to take most corners, but it is right to do so – as will be confirmed in a moment when we examine **Graph 15**.

Now let's imagine a game in which the home team can be expected to score many more goals than the away team – say, 80 per cent of all the goals that are scored. The home team is much better than the away team, even after allowing for ground advantage, which means its attacking play will be much more effective. To score 80 per cent of the goals, it will need to do less than 80 per cent of the attacking, which means it is likely to take less than 80 per cent of the corners.

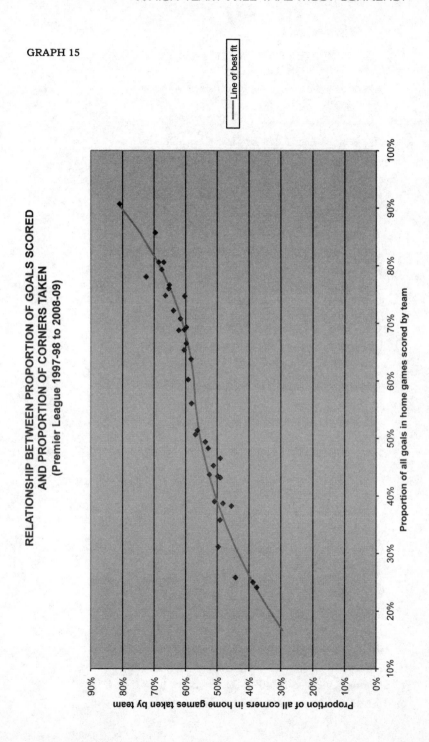

GRAPH 15

RELATIONSHIP BETWEEN PROPORTION OF GOALS SCORED
AND PROPORTION OF CORNERS TAKEN
(Premier League 1997-98 to 2008-09)

Line of best fit

Proportion of all corners in home games taken by team

Proportion of all goals in home games scored by team

COORDINATES FOR LINE OF BEST FIT ON GRAPH 15	
Proportion of all goals in home games scored by team	Proportion of all corners in home games taken by team
24%	38%
26%	40%
28%	42%
30%	43%
32%	45%
34%	47%
36%	48%
38%	49%
40%	51%
42%	52%
44%	53%
46%	54%
48%	55%
50%	55%
52%	56%
54%	57%
56%	57%
58%	57%
60%	57%
62%	58%
64%	58%
66%	59%
68%	60%
70%	61%
72%	62%
74%	63%
76%	65%
78%	67%
80%	68%
82%	70%
84%	72%
86%	75%

Graph 15 has been compiled with data obtained from Premier League games played during the last 12 seasons, 1997-98 to 2008-09. It shows how the proportion of corners for which a home team was

responsible varied with the proportion of goals for which it was responsible.

You will see there is a clear upward trend – the more goals a home team scored, the more corners it was likely to take – but the upward trend is not in a straight line at an angle of 45 degrees. In fact, if you look very closely, you will notice the following things.

We know that overall home teams scored 58 per cent of all goals. If a home team scored more than 58 per cent of the goals, the proportion of goals for which it was responsible was likely to be greater than the proportion of corners for which it was responsible. If a home team scored less than 58 per cent of the goals, the proportion of goals for which it was responsible was likely to be smaller than the proportion of corners for which it was responsible.

If we want to know how corners are likely to be distributed between the teams in a particular match, we need to be able to answer the two questions that were introduced in the last chapter. We need to know what usually happens in this sort of match. And we need to know whether we should be anticipating anything unusual from these two teams. With the help of **Graph 15**, we can now answer the first question, at least for the Premier League, Football League, La Liga, Serie A, Bundesliga and Le Championnat – and with a tolerable degree of accuracy for the Scottish Premier League.

We will attempt to answer the second question in the same way that we have done in previous chapters. Athletes, in common with all other human beings, reveal their characteristics through their behaviour. We can therefore hope to learn something about how they might perform in the future by studying how they have performed in the past. For what proportion of all corners in its games is each team usually responsible? Go back over a period equivalent to roughly a whole season. Ascribe more importance overall to recent displays than distant ones. Take into account games at all venues, both home and away, unless you have a very good reason not to. But, if and where you feel it is appropriate, ignore very occasional outcomes that are both unrepresentative and outlandish.

In our calculations, we should give 38 per cent of the weight to what usually happens in this sort of match and 62 per cent of the weight to what usually happens in the games played by these two teams. And we do so by applying this formula:

$$P_{EHF} = (U_{EHF} \div 100 \times 38) + (J \div (J + K) \times 62)$$

In this formula: P_{EHF} is the proportion of all corners that team E can be expected to take in a game at home to team F; and U_{EHF} is the proportion of all corners that the home team would usually take in a game of this type. We calculate J and K by applying other formulas, which are:

$$J = (50 \times P_E) \div (100 - P_E) \times P_H \div 50$$

$$K = (50 \times P_F) \div (100 - P_F) \times (100 - P_H) \div 50$$

In these formulas: P_E is the proportion of all corners in its games usually taken by team E; P_F is the proportion of all corners in its games usually taken by team F; and P_H is the proportion of all corners in games in that competition usually taken by the home team. In the Premier and Football Leagues, P_H is normally around 57 per cent. It might be easier to comprehend those admittedly rather convoluted equations if you have an example of how they can be put into use. Let's imagine a Premier League game about to be played between team E and team F. We will say that U_{EHF} = 52, P_E = 51, P_F = 43 and P_H = 57.

J = (50 x 51) ÷ (100 - 51) x 57 ÷ 50
  = 59

K = (50 x 43) ÷ (100 - 43) x (100 - 57) ÷ 50
  = 32

So:

P_{EHF} = (52 ÷ 100 x 38) + (59 ÷ (59 + 32) x 62)
  = 60

In other words, team E can be expected to take 60 per cent of all corners against team F – rather more than usual for a home team in a game of that type.

If we know what proportion of all corners in a match a team is likely to gain, we can find out how likely it is to beat or fail to beat a variety of different corner handicaps. We do so by consulting **Graph 16**. Like **Graph 15**, this was compiled with data from games played in the last 12 seasons of the Premier League.

In our example, team E was expected to take 60 per cent of all corners in its game at home to team F. The lines of best fit from **Graph 16** tell us that for team E there is a 65 per cent chance of beating a handicap of -0.5, a 56 per cent chance of beating a handicap of -1.5 and a 47 per cent chance of beating a handicap of -2.5. In other words, team E has a 65 per cent chance of taking more corners than team F (beating a handicap of -0.5), a 56 per cent chance

GRAPH 16

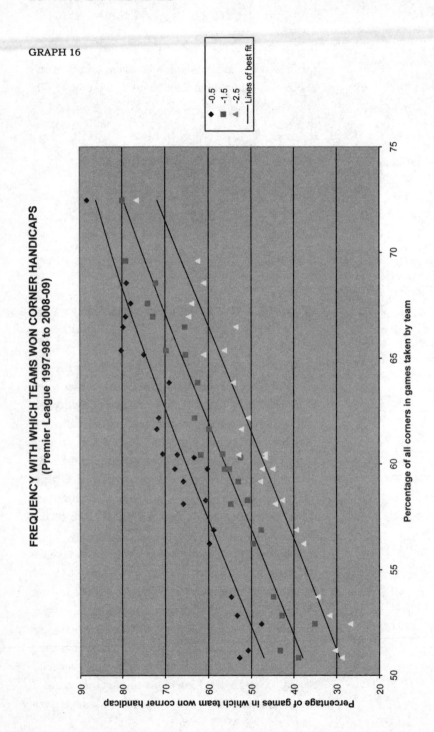

FREQUENCY WITH WHICH TEAMS WON CORNER HANDICAPS
(Premier League 1997-98 to 2008-09)

Percentage of all corners in games taken by team

Percentage of games in which team won corner handicap

- -0.5
- -1.5
- -2.5
- Lines of best fit

COORDINATES FOR LINE OF BEST FIT FOR GRAPH 16						
Percentage of all corners in games taken by team	Percentage of games in which team won selected corner handicap:					
	+0.5	-0.5	-1.5	-2.5	-3.5	-4.5
50	55	45	36	28	20	14
52	59	49	40	31	24	17
54	62	53	44	35	27	20
56	66	57	48	39	30	23
58	70	61	52	43	34	26
60	73	65	56	47	38	29
62	77	69	60	51	42	33
64	80	73	64	55	46	37
66	83	76	68	59	50	40
68	86	79	72	63	54	44
70	88	83	75	67	58	48
72	91	86	79	71	62	53
74	93	88	82	75	66	57
76	94	91	85	78	70	61

NOTE: Columns +0.5, -3.5 and -4.5 not shown on graph

of taking at least two corners more than team F (beating a handicap of -1.5) and a 47 per cent chance of taking at least three corners more than team F (beating a handicap of -2.5). It follows that if there is a 47 per cent chance of team E beating a handicap of -2.5 there must also be a 53 per cent chance of team F beating a handicap of +2.5: 100 - 47 = 53. And so on. If you have forgotten how handicaps work, please refer back to Chapter 5, in which there was a discussion of goal handicaps.

The data in **Graph 16** relates to games in which the average number of corners taken was 11.1. In games in which a higher total is anticipated, the team likely to take most corners would become slightly more likely to beat a handicap of -0.5, -1.5, -2.5 and so on. And vice versa: in games in which a lower total is anticipated, the team likely to take fewest corners would become slightly more likely to beat a handicap of +0.5, +1.5, +2.5 and so on.

In what kinds of corner handicap markets are you most likely to be offered odds that are bigger than they should be? Two kinds, really. First, games involving either one or two teams with a well-established history of exceptional corner splits. To put this into the context of our two basic questions: bookmakers know what usually happens in most sorts of matches, but they do not always know when they should be anticipating something unusual because either or both of the teams has a distinctive playing style. And, secondly, games in which the home team is a very strong favourite to win. What happens here is that bookmakers sometimes overestimate the strength of the favourite's admittedly very impressive attack, and this means they underestimate how much attacking the home team will have to do, which in turn means they underestimate how many corners the home team is likely to take. On such occasions, the team that is most likely to win the match – in fact, overwhelmingly the most likely to win the match – can also be more likely than the odds suggest to beat a corner handicap.

CHAPTER 15

WHO WILL TAKE THE FIRST CORNER?

THE BALANCE OF PLAY ebbs and flows with the score. We learnt this in Chapter 4. A team is more likely to score the next goal if it is losing than if it is drawing, and more likely to score the next goal if it is drawing than if it is winning. What this tells us is that teams do more attacking when they are losing than when they are drawing, and more attacking when they are drawing than when they are winning. And this has implications, among many other things, for the number of corners they get and give away.

In the Premier League during the three seasons from 2006-07 to 2008-09, home teams took 57 per cent of all corners. While scores were level, home teams took 58 per cent of all corners. When they were losing, home teams took 62 per cent of all corners. But when they were winning, home teams took only 51 per cent of all corners.

I think you will agree with me when I say that these figures are very stark. The conclusion I pull from them is that the team that is likely to take most corners in a match is – to put it no higher – at least as likely to take the first corner as it is to take, say, the second corner, the third corner, the fourth corner or any other number that you might care to mention.

Corners are much more plentiful than goals. A referee will point toward a corner flag four or five times as often as he points toward the centre spot after awarding a goal. As corners occur more regularly than goals, they start occurring earlier than goals. In more than five out of every six Premier League games, the first corner arrives before the first goal. In other words, the first corner is almost always taken while the score is still 0-0, which is when the strongest team in the match will be doing more attacking than it might later in the match if it has taken a lead.

You can effectively discount the possibility of no corners being taken. In the 12 seasons from 1997-98 to 2008-09 nearly 25,000 games were played in the Premier and Football Leagues, and not one of them finished without any corners having been taken.

We can therefore say with immense confidence that a team expected to take, say, 65 per cent of all corners in a match has at least a 65 per cent chance of taking the very first corner. And so on for all sorts of different proportions. Yet in matches in which one team is likely to take a very large proportion of all corners bookmakers sometimes underestimate how likely it is to take the first corner. This might be because they know the other team has at least a 50 per cent chance of kicking off and think it could run straight up the pitch and gain a corner. In practice, the initial attack of a match rarely produces a corner.

In the last chapter I said that in matches in which the home team is an overwhelming favourite to score most goals bookmakers will sometimes underestimate how likely it is to take most corners. In matches in which bookmakers do not underestimate how likely that team is to take most corners, they will still sometimes underestimate how likely it is to take the very first corner.

I know that some people are reluctant to bet

on incidental occurrences during a match. And the incidental occurrence on which they are most reluctant to bet is probably the first corner. To them, it seems like an entirely random event but, as I hope I have demonstrated, it is not.

What is betting? It is calculating the chance of something happening and acting accordingly. Or, at least, it should be. The purpose of betting is to try to win money. We can work out the chance of a team taking the first corner, just as we can work out the chance of it doing or not doing many other things during a match – up to and including scoring most goals. All that should matter to us is whether the odds we are being offered about any possibility are bigger than they should be, not what that possibility is.

It is precisely because comparatively few people are prepared to bet on the first corner in a match that bookmakers sometimes pay slightly less attention than they should to setting the odds. Which is not to say that bookmakers are ever careless, still less that winning money from them is ever easy, but it is sometimes not quite so difficult in minor markets as it is in major markets.

CHAPTER 16

HOW MANY CARDS WILL BE SHOWN?

I TOLD YOU THEY WOULD BECOME FAMILIAR. If we want to be able to estimate how many cards will be shown, we will need to be able to answer two questions to which we have become accustomed. What usually happens in this sort of match? And should we be anticipating anything unusual because of today's participants? When betting on bookings, today's participants include not only the teams but also the referee.

The referee does not have as big an influence on the card count as some bettors think, but he does have an influence. As a leading bookmaker once put it to me: "Nobody can punish a foul that is not committed." It is the players, by their behaviour, who either do or do not give the referee disciplinary decisions to make. But, in identical circumstances, different referees would make different decisions.

In card-related markets, most bookmakers award ten points for each yellow and 25 points for each red. The highest number of points that can be allocated to a single player in a match is 35. If he is dismissed for two cautionable offences, the second yellow card, brandished immediately before the red card, is ignored. For betting purposes, he is treated as if he had received one yellow card and then one red card. I have used the same points allocation system for all of the examples in this chapter, and also in the next two chapters as well.

The only cards that count for bookings bets are those shown on the pitch between the first and last whistle. Cards shown before or after the match, or during the half time interval, are ignored. So are cards shown during the match to players or coaches remonstrating from the bench. It is only what happens on the pitch while the match is in progress that is taken into account.

As with corners, so with bookings. We will calculate a bookings points expectation for a match. And then we will convert that bookings points expectation into a percentage chance of different numbers of bookings points being awarded. You will understand by now what is meant by a phrase like bookings points expectation.

Our first question is fairly easy to answer. What usually happens in this sort of match? In most seasons, the average bookings make-up is 36 in the Premier League, 33 in the Football League, 37 in the Scottish Premier League, 62 in La Liga, 52 in Serie A, 43 in the Bundesliga and 40 in Le Championnat. It is 39 in the Champions League.

Fans in different countries prefer to watch different styles of football. And – though the fans themselves would probably not accept the truth of this assertion – referees try to give them what they want. In England, for example, the most frequently heard complaint about referees is that they whistle too often. Yet English referees blow for fewer fouls, fewer yellow cards and fewer red cards than their counterparts in any other major football nation in Europe. And they do this even though English football tends to be more violent, not less violent, than the version played elsewhere in Europe.

One word of warning before we move on. I will

elaborate on it later in this chapter. You should always be sensitive to the atmosphere in which a game is likely to be played, because this will influence the behaviour of the players. In an emotion-charged local derby, for instance, you should anticipate rather more yellow and red cards than you would on another day if these fierce rivals were not playing each other.

So what about our second question? Should we be anticipating anything unusual because of today's participants? Is either or both of the teams conspicuously well behaved or badly behaved? Is the referee particularly lenient or strict? We will try to find out by looking at what happened in games in which they were involved in the past. I would suggest the now customary kind of research. Go back over a period equivalent to roughly a whole season, at the very least. Attach more importance overall to recent games than to distant ones. Take into account all games, both home and away.

You might wonder why we are interested in all bookings points awarded during a team's games – not only the bookings points accumulated by that team but also the bookings points accumulated by its opponents. The reason is that footballers, like all other human beings, can influence one another. If somebody is nice to us, we are more likely than we would otherwise have been to behave nicely toward them. If somebody is nasty to us, we are more likely than we would otherwise have been to behave nastily toward them.

It's the same on the football pitch as it is anywhere else. If somebody kicks you on the ankle, your instinctive reaction might be to spin round and kick them on the ankle, too. If somebody knocks you to the ground accidentally but apologises profusely and then helps you to your feet, you might accept their expression of regret, shake hands and play on. Well-behaved teams tend to encourage better than normal behaviour from their opponents, and badly behaved teams tend to provoke worse than normal behaviour from their opponents. In other words, a team with perfectly ordinary disciplinary habits is likely to receive fewer yellow and red cards in games against well-behaved opponents than it does in games against badly behaved opponents.

In the Premier League, referees are involved in an average of 18 or 19 games per season, about half as many as a team. I would therefore suggest that when assessing what to anticipate from an official you should be prepared to go back over more than one whole season.

And how do we calculate what the bookings expectation should be for a match? I will be perfectly honest with you, which is what I have always tried to do. The equations you have to apply are not entirely straightforward. You might find it easier to follow the calculation process if we split it into two parts. In the first part, we will calculate what the bookings points expectation should be without any reference to the referee. Or, if you prefer, we will be assuming that the referee is absolutely typical of officials in that competition. In the second part, we will allow for the influence, one way or the other, of the man who is actually going to be in the middle.

We will use the term B_{YZ} to describe our initial bookings points expectation for a match to be played between teams Y and Z without any reference to the referee.

$$B_{YZ} = (B_Y \times B_Z \div B_D \times 0.72) + (B_D \times 0.28)$$

In this equation, B_Y is the number of bookings points usually awarded in the games of team Y, B_Z is the number of bookings points usually awarded in the games of team Z, and B_D is the number of bookings points usually awarded in games in that competition.

We must now allow for the influence of the referee. We will use the term B_{YZR} to describe our final bookings points expectation for a match to be played between teams Y and Z with referee R.

$$B_{YZR} = (B_{YZ} \times 0.48) + (B_{YZ} \times B_R \div B_D \times 0.52)$$

In this equation, B_R is the number of bookings points usually awarded in the games of referee R.

Let's put some figures into those formulas. Let's imagine a Premier League game about to be played between teams Y and Z with referee R. We will say that B_Y is 32, B_Z is 44, B_R is 45 and B_D is 36. In other words, our game features one well-behaved team, one badly behaved team and a disciplinarian referee.

$$B_{YZ} = (32 \times 44 \div 36 \times 0.72) + (36 \times 0.28) = 38$$

So:

$$B_{YZR} = (38 \times 0.48) + (38 \times 45 \div 36 \times 0.52) = 43$$

Our bookings points expectation for the match therefore becomes 43.

Ultimately, what we really want to know, of course, is the percentage chance of the make-up today being 0, 10, 20 and so on. **Graph 17** tells us. It shows the relationship, in the Premier League during the last 12 seasons, between the average number of bookings

GRAPH 17

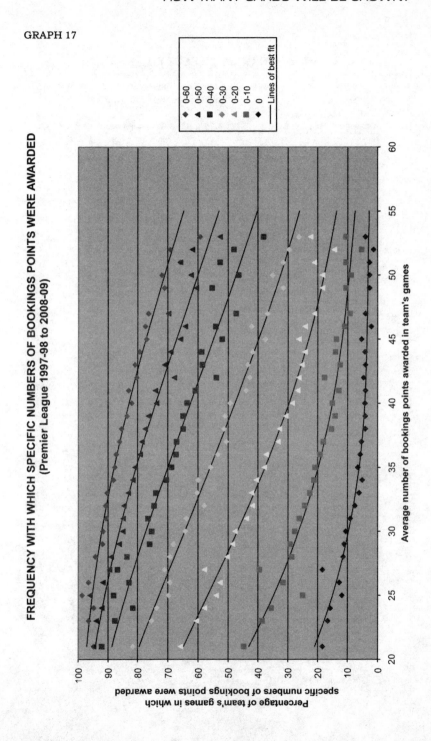

FREQUENCY WITH WHICH SPECIFIC NUMBERS OF BOOKINGS POINTS WERE AWARDED
(Premier League 1997-98 to 2008-09)

Legend:
- 0-60 ◆
- 0-50 ◀
- 0-40 ■
- 0-30 ◆
- 0-20 ◀
- 0-10 ■
- 0 ◆
- Lines of best fit

Y-axis: Percentage of team's games in which specific numbers of bookings points were awarded

X-axis: Average number of bookings points awarded in team's games

COORDINATES FOR LINES OF BEST FIT ON GRAPH 17										
Average number of bookings points awarded in team's games	Percentage of team's games in which specific number of bookings points were awarded:									
	0	0-10	0-20	0-25	0-30	0-35	0-40	0-45	0-50	0-55	0-60
21	21	43	65	65	79	81	89	90	94	96	97
22	19	41	63	63	78	79	88	89	93	95	97
23	18	39	61	61	76	77	86	88	93	94	96
24	16	37	59	59	75	76	85	87	92	94	96
25	15	35	57	57	73	74	84	86	91	93	95
26	14	33	55	55	71	72	83	85	90	92	95
27	13	31	53	53	70	71	81	83	89	91	94
28	12	29	51	51	68	69	80	82	88	91	93
29	10	28	49	49	66	67	79	81	87	90	93
30	10	26	47	47	64	66	77	79	86	89	92
31	9	25	45	45	63	64	76	78	85	88	91
32	8	24	43	43	61	62	74	76	84	87	91
33	7	22	41	42	59	60	73	75	83	86	90
34	7	21	39	40	58	59	71	74	82	85	89
35	6	20	38	38	56	57	70	72	80	83	88
36	6	19	36	36	54	55	68	70	79	82	87
37	5	18	34	35	53	54	67	69	78	81	86
38	5	17	33	33	51	52	65	67	77	80	85
39	4	16	31	31	49	50	64	66	75	78	84
40	4	15	30	30	48	49	62	64	74	77	83
41	4	14	28	28	46	47	61	63	73	76	82
42	4	14	27	27	45	45	59	61	71	74	81
43	4	13	25	26	43	44	58	59	70	73	80
44	4	12	24	24	41	42	56	58	68	72	78
45	3	12	23	23	40	41	55	56	67	70	77
46	3	11	22	22	38	39	53	55	66	69	76
47	3	11	21	21	37	37	52	53	64	67	75
48	3	10	20	20	35	36	50	52	63	66	74
49	3	10	19	19	34	35	49	50	61	64	72
50	3	9	18	18	33	33	47	48	60	63	71
51	3	9	17	17	31	32	46	47	59	61	70
52	3	9	16	16	30	30	44	46	57	60	68
53	3	8	15	15	29	29	43	44	56	58	67
54	3	8	14	15	27	28	42	43	54	57	66
55	3	7	14	14	26	27	40	41	53	55	65

NOTE: Columns 0-25, 0-35, 0-45 and 0-55 not shown on graph

Alan Wiley expels Manchester United's Nemanja Vidic

points in a team's games and the percentage of that team's games in which the make-up was 0, 0-10, 0-20 and so on.

We have imagined a game in which the bookings points expectation is 43. The lines of best fit on Graph 17 tell us the following – that there is a four per cent chance of a make-up of 0, a 13 per cent chance of a make-up of 0-10, a 25 per cent chance of a make-up of 0-20, a 43 per cent chance of make-up of 0-30, a 58 per cent chance of a make-up of 0-40, a 70 per cent chance of a make-up of 0-50 and an 80 per cent chance of a make-up of 0-60.

We can manipulate those figures in the same way that we have manipulated other figures from other graphs in other chapters. If, for example, there is a 13 per cent chance of a make-up no higher than 10 and a 25 per cent chance of a make-up no higher than 20, there must be a 12 per cent chance of a make-up of exactly 10 (25 - 13 = 12). And so on, for all sorts of other possibilities.

I said earlier that you should always be sensitive to the atmosphere in which a game is likely to be played. If Everton are playing Liverpool, there is no point in wasting your time trying to work out how many cards have been issued in Everton's games against other opponents or in Liverpool's games against other opponents. Today they are not playing anyone else. They are playing each other.

In the Premier League during the last 12 seasons, the average bookings make-up in Everton's games was 39 and in Liverpool's games it was 35. The average make-up when they played each other in Merseyside derbies was 62. The average make-up in North London derbies between Arsenal and Tottenham was 50.

In the five seasons from 2004-05 to 2008-09, the Premier League was dominated by a so-called Big Four of Arsenal, Chelsea, Liverpool and Manchester United. When they played other opponents, the average bookings make-up was 36. When they played each other, it was 50 – approximately 40 per cent higher. You should always ask yourself whether the game a team is about to play is like most of the others that it has played in the past. If it is not, be prepared to revise your bookings expectations dramatically. The normal calculations can hardly ever be applied to abnormal contests.

The more that is at stake during a game the more likely it is that tempers will become frayed. A curious exception, however, must be made for set piece occasions at prestigious neutral venues. In cup finals, for example, our bookings points expectations should generally be no higher than they would have been if the two teams had been playing each other in a league fixture. This might be because referees do not want to be criticised for spoiling the occasion by issuing too many cards, or because players, for all that they want to win, still have some respect for that occasion – or some combination of the two. The average bookings make up in FA Cup finals is 35. In Champions League finals it is 38.

About what sort of proposition are you most likely to be offered odds that are bigger than they should be? In all sorts of matches, in all sorts of competitions, in all sorts of countries, the answer will be the same: bets on low numbers of bookings points.

The respected football journalist Patrick Barclay once wrote of his disgust at watching a match on a big screen in a London bar surrounded by City boys who spent the entire 90 minutes braying for the referee to book players. He would probably be equally disgusted to be told that it is possible to make money over time by betting in the opposite way to such people.

If they bet on bookings, nearly everybody bets on a high total. They want a bet that will be fun to watch. And it is no fun at all to sit through a match hoping every time a player launches into a tackle that he will not connect with his opponent – or that, if he does, he will be excused by the referee. In a typical Premier League match there are 26 fouls. You will suffer 26 heart-stopping moments as you wait to see whether the referee reaches for his cards. And you will suffer many, many more spasms of anxiety – one every time a player commits himself, or appears to be about to commit himself, to a tackle.

It is because bookmakers find it so hard to sell bets on low numbers of bookings that they will sometimes quote you a price that is better than it should be.

CHAPTER 17

WHICH TEAM WILL RECEIVE MOST BOOKINGS?

REFEREES, ON THE WHOLE, are not intimidated by the noise from a crowd. Most football followers think they are. It is fairly easy to show that they are not.

Inside any ground during almost any game, most spectators will be cheering for the home team. If referees were intimidated by the roar from the crowd, they would punish players from the away team for offences for which they would not punish players from the home team – which is, of course, an accusation levelled against them. It does not happen – or, at least, if it does, it must happen only very rarely.

A player can be shown a yellow card for any one of these reasons: unsporting conduct, dissent, persistent infringement, delaying a restart, encroachment at a corner, free kick or throw in, entering or leaving the pitch without permission. He can be shown a red card for any one of these reasons: serious foul play, violent conduct, spitting, denying an obvious goalscoring opportunity, use of offensive, insulting or abusive language or gestures, and being guilty of a second cautionable offence.

In theory, any player could be shown a card in

almost any match situation. In practice, cards are almost always shown to a defender following a failed attempt to regain the ball. In other words, cards are normally a consequence of defence. The more defending a team does the more fouls it will commit and the more yellow and red cards it will collect.

In the Premier League during the last 12 seasons – 1997-98 to 2008-09 – away teams conceded 58 per cent of all goals and accumulated 58 per cent of all bookings points. In other words, there was an exact correspondence between the amount of defending they were required to do and the number of yellow and red cards they received in the process.

I think this shows pretty clearly that referees, considered collectively, are not cowed by the howling mob pouring vitriol down upon them from the stands. Overall, away teams do receive more cards than home teams, but this is only because they do more defending than home teams.

As the volume of defending that a team is likely to do goes up or down, so does the number of bookings points it is likely to receive. By how much? Graph 18 tells us. It shows the relationship in the Premier League during the last 12 seasons between the proportion of goals for which a team was responsible in its home games and the proportion of bookings points for which that team was responsible in its home games. It is pretty much a mirror image of Graph 15, which depicted the relationship between goals and corners. You can re-examine Graph 15 by flicking back to page 119.

We now know how bookings points are usually split between the teams in all sorts of different matches. If we are trying to anticipate what will happen in a particular match that is about to be played, we will also want to know whether we should modify our

GRAPH 18

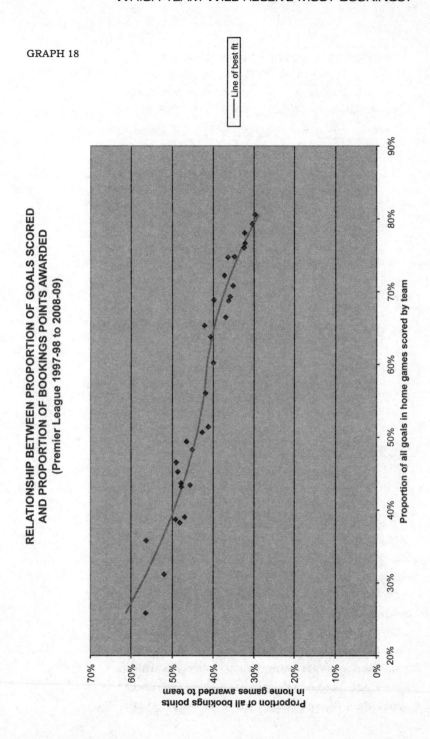

RELATIONSHIP BETWEEN PROPORTION OF GOALS SCORED
AND PROPORTION OF BOOKINGS POINTS AWARDED
(Premier League 1997-98 to 2008-09)

Line of best fit

Proportion of all goals in home games scored by team

Proportion of all bookings points
in home games awarded to team

COORDINATES FOR LINE OF BEST FIT ON GRAPH 18	
Proportion of all goals in home games scored by team	Proportion of all bookings points in home games awarded to team
26%	61%
28%	59%
30%	57%
32%	56%
34%	54%
36%	52%
38%	51%
40%	50%
42%	48%
44%	47%
46%	46%
48%	45%
50%	44%
52%	43%
54%	43%
56%	42%
58%	42%
60%	42%
62%	41%
64%	40%
66%	39%
68%	38%
70%	37%
72%	36%
74%	35%
76%	33%
78%	31%
80%	29%

expectations in any way because of the disciplinary habits of the participating teams.

We find out by a now familiar method. Establish what has happened in the games played by each team over a period equivalent to roughly a whole season. Attribute more significance overall to recent games than distant ones. Include all games, both home and away. But be prepared, if and when you feel it is appropriate, to ignore rare outcomes that were both unrepresentative and outlandish.

We can work out precisely how the bookings points are likely to be apportioned when the two teams play each other by applying the following formulas:

$$P_{YHZ} = (U_{YHZ} \div 100 \times 38) + (S \div (S + T) \times 62)$$

In this formula: P_{YHZ} is the proportion of all bookings points that team Y can be expected to receive in a game at home to team Z; and U_{YHZ} is the proportion of all bookings points that the home team would usually receive in a game of this type. We calculate S and T by applying other formulas, which are:

$$S = (50 \times P_Y) \div (100 - P_Y) \times P_H \div 50$$

$$T = (50 \times P_Z) \div (100 - P_Z) \times (100 - P_H) \div 50$$

In these formulas: P_Y is the proportion of all bookings points in its games usually received by team Y; P_Z is the proportion of all bookings points in its games usually received by team Z; and P_H is the proportion of all bookings points in games in that competition usually received by the home team. In the Premier and Football Leagues, P_H is normally around 42 per cent. In our calculations, we are giving 38 per cent of the weight to what usually happens in this sort of match and 62 per cent of the weight to what usually happens in the matches played by these two teams – having tested countless alternatives over the years, I have come to the conclusion that these weights are the ones that produce the most accurate forecasts.

We can now move on to **Graph 19**, which tells us how often teams won, drew and lost bookings points

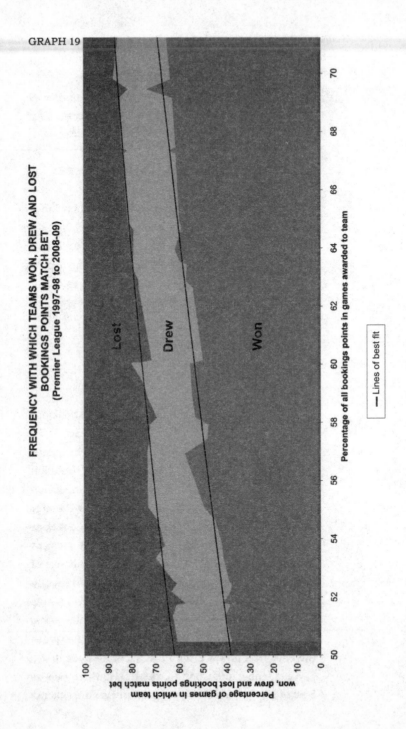

GRAPH 19

FREQUENCY WITH WHICH TEAMS WON, DREW AND LOST
BOOKINGS POINTS MATCH BET
(Premier League 1997-98 to 2008-09)

Lost

Drew

Won

— Lines of best fit

Percentage of all bookings points in games awarded to team

Percentage of games in which team
won, drew and lost bookings points match bet

COORDINATES FOR LINES OF BEST FIT ON GRAPH 19			
Percentage of all bookings points in games awarded to team	Percentage of games in which team won, drew and lost bookings points match bet:		
	Won	Drew	Lost
50	38.1	23.8	38.1
51	39.8	23.8	36.5
52	41.3	23.7	35.0
53	42.9	23.5	33.6
54	44.4	23.4	32.2
55	45.9	23.2	30.9
56	47.4	23.1	29.5
57	48.9	22.9	28.3
58	50.4	22.6	27.0
59	51.8	22.4	25.8
60	53.3	22.1	24.6
61	54.7	21.8	23.4
62	56.1	21.6	22.3
63	57.6	21.2	21.2
64	59.0	20.9	20.1
65	60.4	20.6	19.1
66	61.7	20.2	18.1
67	63.1	19.8	17.1
68	64.4	19.4	16.1
69	65.8	19.0	15.2
70	67.1	18.6	14.3
71	68.4	18.2	13.4
72	69.6	17.8	12.6

match bets – that is to say, how often they received more, the same number or fewer bookings points than their opponents. **Graph 19** illustrates what happened during the last 12 seasons of the Premier League.

If we know what percentage of bookings points in a match a team can be expected to gain – and now we do – **Graph 19** will tell us the percentage chance of that team receiving more, the same number or fewer bookings points than its opponents. Or, at least, it will for what we can call standard games in the Premier League. The average bookings points make-up in the

Premier League is 36. In games in which more than 36 bookings points are anticipated, the prospect of both teams receiving the same number will be lower than indicated by **Graph 19** – and the prospect of one team receiving more than another will be higher. The opposite is also true: in games in which fewer than 36 bookings points are anticipated, the prospect of both teams receiving the same number will be higher than indicated by Graph 19 – and the prospect of one team receiving more than another will be lower.

In my experience, bookmakers sometimes underestimate the possibility of both teams receiving the same number of bookings points, particularly in games in which the total number of bookings points awarded is likely to be low. Very few thrill-of-the-moment bettors will back the tie – for bookings any more than goals – and the low demand for such bets can over-inflate the price.

You will sometimes discover other possibilities being offered at odds that are bigger than they should be. Bookmakers occasionally fail to spot teams who have a well-established habit of accumulating either a much larger or much smaller share of the bookings points than others with a similar playing strength. Generally speaking, bookmakers know what usually happens in most sorts of matches. They do not always know when they should be anticipating something unusual because one or all of the participants has highly distinctive characteristics. You do.

CHAPTER 18

WHO WILL RECEIVE THE FIRST CARD?

WE EVALUATE THE PROSPECT OF A TEAM receiving the first card in the same way that we evaluate the prospect of it scoring the first goal or taking the first corner. You already know everything that you need to know to be able to do this.

Suppose team A is about to play team B in the Premier League. You think team A should be expected to accumulate 42 per cent of all bookings points and team B 58 per cent. Your bookings points expectation for the whole match is 36. If you refer back to Graph 17 on page 135, you will find that in a match with a bookings points expectation of 36 there is a 6 per cent chance of no bookings points at all being issued. In other words, there is a 94 per cent chance (100 - 6 = 94) of at least one card being issued.

The percentage chance of team A receiving the first card is effectively this:

42 ÷ 100 x 94 = 39

The percentage chance of team B receiving the first card is effectively this:

58 ÷ 100 x 94 = 55

The games that are likely to offer value for money

in first card markets are the same as those that are likely to offer value for money in most card markets – that is to say, games involving teams who have a well established pattern of attracting either a much larger or much smaller share of all bookings than others with a similar playing strength. The possibility of no cards being issued can be underestimated as well.

The commonest subjects of football bets are goals, corners and bookings. As I have said before, you will be examined on one of two questions, which can be phrased in a great variety of different ways. How many will there be? And how will they be distributed between the teams? In the first half of this book we learnt how to answer those questions for goals. In the second half we have learnt how to answer them for corners and bookings. It is now time to bring everything together.

CONCLUSION

APPARENTLY, THE SUCCESSFUL GAMBLER HARRY FINDLAY once doubted whether anyone could make a profit of more than eight per cent on turnover. Another successful gambler, Patrick Veitch, who was quoted at the start of this book, has managed a higher figure – but one that is still in the teens.

What does this tell you? It tells me that even the very best bettors of them all win only slightly more money than they lose. And that has important implications for the ways in which we should go about trying to emulate them.

Let's imagine three things – that you are one of the best bettors in the world, that over time you will make a profit of eight per cent on your turnover, and that the average of all the prices at which you bet is evens.

You can expect to win 54 per cent of your bets and lose 46 per cent of your bets. But your wins and losses will not occur in neat, regular patterns. No way. If you placed one bet every day for a year, it is more likely than not that you would experience at least one seven day period in which all of your bets lost. And there would be many more times when you suffered six losses, five losses, or four. In other words, there would be a great number of seven day periods in which you lost more money than you won.

And, remember, you are one of the best bettors in the world.

You can begin to see that even very good bettors will endure losing runs, some of which will be very long indeed – and, it should be added, for the sake of completeness, even very bad bettors will enjoy winning runs, some of which will also be very long indeed. Whichever you are, you should be prepared, financially and psychologically, to withstand all of the many vagaries of betting.

Imagine two people who are new to gambling. One loses their first ten bets. The other wins their first ten bets. Is the first person a very bad bettor? Or are they perhaps a very good bettor who has just been unlucky enough to start with a terrible sequence of results? Or maybe something in between? And what about the second person? Are they are a very good bettor? Or perhaps a very bad bettor who has just been lucky enough to start with a terrific sequence of results? Or something in between?

The truth is that we don't know and neither do they. Such things will only become clear with time. It is therefore highly desirable that both of them should bet in such a way that they are able to stay in the game long enough to find out.

I would suggest two things to start with. The first is that you set aside money for a betting bank and keep it separate from all of your other money. The best way to do this is to put it into a different account.

The second thing is that you should only ever risk a small portion of your betting bank on any individual bet. It is often said that people should bet only with money they can afford to lose, and this is good advice as far as it goes. I would take it further and say that you should not only be able to afford to lose this bet, but that afterwards you should be able to afford to lose a large number of other bets as well, all in a row. You will then have the peace of mind that comes from knowing that you could probably survive even an inordinately long losing run.

It is hard enough to find good bets. Don't make it harder by piling pressure on yourself, because this will impair your judgement. And you would be piling pressure on yourself if you ever allowed yourself to get into a position where you could not afford to lose your next few bets – or, worst of all, just the next bet.

Stake more on strong fancies than on less strong fancies, and more at short odds than at long odds. On a strongly fancied bet at even money I would risk ten times as much as I would on a strongly fancied bet at 10-1. Over time I would hope that both types of bet would generate a similar level of profit – and I would not have to fear either type of bet exposing me to a greater risk of bankruptcy.

We have already touched on some of the psychological aspects of gambling and now we will touch on some more. Whether you are on a winning sequence or a losing sequence, you should always try to select and stake your bets in exactly the same way. It is easy to say but – to put it mildly – not easy to do.

In a popular poem, Rudyard Kipling said that we should be able to "meet with Triumph and Disaster and treat those two impostors just the same". We should aspire to that ideal, even though we will never reach it, because along the way we might at least acquire a better sense of perspective than we have at the moment. And without a very good sense of perspective indeed, anyone who bets will swiftly degenerate into an emotional wreck.

In other lines from that famous poem, Kipling said that you should "trust yourself when all men doubt you, but make allowance for their doubting too". When you find yourself on a losing run, review the bets you have been placing and ask yourself whether there are any relevant, result-influencing factors that bookmakers have been taking into account but you have been overlooking. If there are, you will have learnt from your losses and can stop making them. If not, swallow hard and press on.

It is better, of course, to spot your mistakes before placing your bets rather than afterwards. It is not always possible – there will always be losing runs and there will always be the need for reviews – but it is sometimes possible. I therefore suggest that before placing any bet you should ask yourself a very straightforward question: "why is this person offering me odds that are bigger than I think they should be?"

He – it almost certainly will be a he – is probably a knowledgeable and experienced odds-setter. He might have made a mistake. It is conceivable. But it is more likely that he has a reason. What is it? If you know why this person is quoting these odds, and, having reflected dispassionately, you are convinced his reasoning is wrong, then you can go ahead and place the bet with great confidence. Whether you win or lose on this particular occasion doesn't really matter. You are entitled to feel that if all of your bets are like this then you will eventually win more money than you lose. If you don't know why this person is quoting these odds, I would suggest you pause.

The legendary poker player Amarillo Slim once said: "Decisions, not results. Do the right thing enough times and the results will take care of themselves in the long run." Right at the beginning of this book, I said that if you wanted to win money consistently by betting on football you would need to know two things – what the odds should be and where you might find odds that are wrong. The purpose of this book has been to help you acquire that knowledge. In short, to make the right decisions.

Index

Victor Chandler
SPORTS · CASINO · POKER · GAMES

£100 FREE
TO ALL NEW CASINO
CUSTOMERS

victorchandler.com